THE COLLECTED POETRY OF
ALDOUS HUXLEY

A ⟨signature⟩ BOOK

BOOKS BY ALDOUS HUXLEY

NOVELS

Island
The Genius and the Goddess
Ape and Essence
Time Must Have a Stop
*After Many a Summer Dies
   the Swan*
Eyeless in Gaza
Point Counter Point
Those Barren Leaves
Antic Hay
Crome Yellow
Brave New World

ESSAYS AND
BELLES LETTRES

On Art and Artists
Collected Essays
Brave New World Revisted
*Tomorrow and Tomorrow
   and Tomorrow*
Heaven and Hell
The Doors of Perception
The Devils of Loudun
Themes and Variations
Ends and Means
Texts and Pretexts
The Olive Tree
Music at Night
Vulgarity in Literature
Do What You Will
Proper Studies
Jesting Pilate
Along the Road
On the Margin
Essays New and Old
The Art of Seeing
The Perennial Philosophy
Science, Liberty and Peace

SHORT STORIES

Collected Short Stories
Brief Candles
Two or Three Graces
Limbo
Little Mexican
Mortal Coils

BIOGRAPHY

Grey Eminence

POETRY

The Cicadas
Leda

TRAVEL

Beyond the Mexique Bay

DRAMA

Mortal Coils—A Play
The World of Light
*The Discovery, adapted from
   Frances Sheridan*

SELECTED WORKS

Rotunda
The World of Aldous Huxley
Letters of Aldous Huxley
*The Collected Poetry of
   Aldous Huxley*

THE
COLLECTED POETRY
OF
ALDOUS HUXLEY

EDITED BY
DONALD WATT

With an Introduction by
RICHARD CHURCH

HARPER & ROW, PUBLISHERS
New York, Evanston, San Francisco, London

Contents

Introduction by Richard Church   7

1 The Burning Wheel (1916)   13

2 The Defeat of Youth and Other Poems (1918)   39

3 Leda (1920)   81

4 The Cicadas and Other Poems (1931)   129

   Title Index   167

Introduction

Aldous Huxley was born in 1894 and died in 1963. For most of his life he was almost blind, but like another, younger scholar and poet, John Heath Stubbs, through sheer force of character and intellectual ability, he converted this physical deterrent into an incentive. His achieved mental and moral vision made him the most caustic critic of the hysteria of the post-war Western World in the 1920's and subsequent decades. It carried farther, later in his courageous life, to a more mystical vision, compassionate, all-embracing, through every religious creed and mythology where he could trace the pure gold of virtue and a recipe for loving-kindness.

His career thus falls into two periods. First he lacerated society, then he set out to heal it of its self-inflicted wounds. He was most widely influential toward this purpose through his prose. His novels, essays, accounts of his experiments in psychological exploration are world-famous, and have played a large part in shaping conduct, ideas, manners. His medicine has been astringent.

So large has been this aspect of his life and work, that another side of his personality has tended to be overlooked. It has found expression in a comparatively small body of poetry, which is here collected for the first time in one volume. Readers will appreciate that this is almost a foreign interruption into a family tradition of cool, scientific approach to the problems of life, death and continuity. His grandfather was the spokesman for Darwin's modest but world-shaking challenge to the myth which has been the basis of every religion's account of the origin of the universe. His elder brother Julian is an eminent scientist also gifted, like that grandfather, with the power of incisive and graceful literary expression.

Aldous inherited all these qualities, but added something of his own. It was a more cleanly detached craving for command of the magic of words; the aspiration of a poet. He published his first book of verse in 1916, during the First World War when there was a sudden revival of interest in poetry. The first poem in that collection voices the disturbances of mind of a man of twenty, questioning the environment in which he had been brought up, as he saw it threatened by the holocaust which was beginning to rage and to consume both the physical and emotional acceptances of a comparatively complacent century.

> "Wearied of its own turning,
> Distressed with its own busy restlessness,
> Yearning to draw the circumferent pain –
> The rim that is dizzy with speed –
> To the motionless centre, there to rest,
> The wheel must strain through agony
> On agony contracting, returning
> Into the core of steel."

That was the beginning of his large output of prophetic utterance. The return to the core of steel is still in process over half a century later. This young man, saved by his near blindness from the doom of a decimal of his generation, was already so self-disciplined that he could see the potential destructiveness of that "core of steel".

But his disability was already an asset, for it determined a physical enclosure of poetic imagery, and thus the idiom of his thinking. But throughout his verse the consciousness of this special non-equipment sometimes finds direct expression. See, for instance, the poem "Mole" and compare it with Milton's sonnet on his blindness. Both poems challenge the physical fatality. Milton declares that "they also serve who only stand and wait". Aldous proposes to

> ".............. tunnel on and on
> Till night let fall oblivion."

This evidence of a resolute spirit, stated at the very beginning of his career, is a kind of key-signature to all his writings. It is the tone which is

> "Passed down the long line to the last that bears
> The name, a gift of yearnings and despairs
> Too greatly noble for this iron age."

8

He says that about the character of Villiers de l'Isle-Adam, one of the many French poets whose work he explored while seeking his own idiom in the making of verse. He read, what in the teens of the century was fashionable here through Arthur Symons's and Eliot's recommendation, the French Symbolistes, from which stemmed our Imagiste group: F. S. Flint, Richard Aldington, "H.D.", Ford Madox Ford, Herbert Read and others. But Aldous did not reject the luxuries of the Romantics, whose preoccupation with visual inspiration had been microscopically focused by the pre-Raphaelites. Maybe his defective sight alarmed him into this, as a compensatory move. The early poems are obsessed with this struggle to *see* the world around him. The effort is like that of a man drowning. Aldous reaches the shore; but it is not that of *our* exterior world.

We find him turning inward, to the continents of the mind. How he contrived the scholastic approach remains a miracle of will-power and its ingenuities.

> "Old ghosts that death forgot to ferry
> Across the Lethe of the years ...
> These are my friends, and at their tears
> I weep and with their mirth am merry"

Yet in spite of this enforced, more than myopic removal from his visual inheritance, he snatches poetry from it, as in the sestet from a sonnet called "The Canal".

> "Between unseeing walls the waters rest,
> Lifeless and hushed, till suddenly a swan
> Glides from some broader river blue as day,
> And with the mirrored magic of his breast
> Creates within that barren water-way
> New life, new loveliness, and passes on."

His outbreaks of impatience and rebellion against his handicap become increasingly expressed in verse suggestive of the idiom of T. S. Eliot, another disorientated figure destined to make his mark during the breaking of our civilization. Aldous cries out, more in the key of his future prose

> " .... The tinkling rain
> Of that small sentimental music wets

Your parching suburb: it may sprout . . . who knows? . . .
In something red and silken like a rose,
In sheaves of almost genuine violets."

This carries a warning of the post-war conflict of the 1920's;
the sub-anger, the sense of cheat, after Lloyd George's prom-
ises of a world fit for heroes. Aldous sees the heroes maimed,
and the cravens flourishing on the ruins of idealism and religious
faith. Yet romantic love between man and woman blows, with
springtime fragrance, through this tumbled scene

"And love flows in on him, its vastness pent
Within his narrow life".

His narrow life! This is the moment to notice a quality which
emerges in his verse. It is something hardly consonant with his
general reputation as a sophisticated intellectual, the ruthless
critic whose novels were to set the mode of iconoclasm which
was to hammer the tottering institutions still left standing after
1918: the social conventions and pretensions, the religious
dogmas, the outmoded formulas of science.
This quality is innocence, a difficult word to define. It is the
rare possession which in maturity develops, if it survives at all,
into a sixth sense whose attributes are hyper-intuition, saintly
insight, spiritual interpretation. Eventually, this inherited but
latent gene, which promoted the habit of courtesy in all mem-
bers of the Huxley family, commanded Aldous's whole character as man and writer. It made him turn against the tide of
fashion in literature and philosophy. He was no longer the
popular iconoclast of the Western World. It was to lead to his
deeply religious explorations in *The Perennial Philosophy*.
In his poetry, it took up the usual melancholy unrest of
adolescent yearnings and made it an incandescence, such as
shone from the best of Shelley's uneven poetry, and in Matthew
Arnold's noble pessimism, where despair is committed by
divine paradox into faith and a fuller consciousness of the
rumbling workings of the universe, beyond "where ignorant
armies clash by night".
Under this authority henceforth, Aldous, in his poetry, and
despite his defective eyes, sees

> "Noonday upon the Alpine meadows
> Pour its avalanche of Light".

This illumination was to lead him to another world. As he wrote,

> "There is a country in my mind
> Lovelier than a poet blind
> Could dream of, who had never known
> This world of drought and dust and stone
> In all its ugliness.........."

This transfer of authority, however, produced some disturbance of aesthetic control. Some of the verse *welters*, both in imagery and rhythm, as in the poem "Valedictory" (pages 63-4). The conflict in his personality was not yet fully abated, and I suspect it has been the disturbing element in his writings, both in verse and prose, which prevents them from possessing the simplicity and hardness of perfect form. Sometimes, under this distress, his work is in bad taste. The "Love Song" following "Valedictory" is a grim example. Readers of the novels will recall similar instances, horrid interruptions of exalted planes of thought and feeling, catastrophic between strophe and antistrophe of an almost Aeschylean interchange of vocal balance.

He was too intelligent to be unaware of this weakness, and he openly derided it in his *"Complaint of a Poet Manqué"* (page 69). Much of the verse in this volume of *Collected Poetry* shows the uncertainty and torment of a man still struggling to release his unique spiritual maturity. He cries out

> "But a time came when, turning full of hate
> And weariness from my remembered themes,
> I wished my poet's pipe could modulate
> Beauty more palpable than words and dreams."

Such utterances as that are of more value to the biographer than to the literary critic, though they throw some light into the declivities which occur in all his work, with the exception of the masterpiece *The Perennial Philosophy*, where his running commentary linking the anthology is flawless.

So in his longest and most ambitious poem "Leda", a retelling in rhymed couplets of one of the Greek forms of the myth of an

Immaculate Conception, the dichotomy of his personality is apparent. Here is a poem with the sensuous texture of Keats's "Lamia", but a Keats with interjections from a training at Balliol, almost making the innocence self-conscious. A friend who was killed in 1918 wrote to him five weeks before that death and said, "I doubt whether your verses will be so very much more perennial than brass. Still, they'll be something."

It remains for the reader today to decide about that pre-mortuary prophecy. We know, from the evidence of the rest of Huxley's career, how he emerged from brass to gold. The interest in these poems is to isolate that gold, as a promissory vein of the spiritual riches which this rare and courteous man, of incredible bravery, revealed as both critical and prophetic wealth to the Western World, and to the threatened human race in its entirety.

Aldous wrote, in response to that early criticism, a long poem which reveals the whole man, as poet and living (as distinct from linguistic) philosopher. The dichotomy is reconciled, with his discovery of "The life so short, so vast love's science and art."

Brassiness is the quality one may attribute to the period of the 1920's, to include the Bloomsbury Group; but we know from Aldous Huxley's complete development, that his personal vein of poetry was not brassy, but golden, even though more clearly revealed in prose than verse. Yet its most original proclamation is found in the long poem written in reply to that dead friend's challenge, and entitled "Soles Occidere et Redire Possunt".

The complete fusion of all his attributes, including even the physical deprivation due to semi-blindness, comes in the powerful poem "The Cicadas". It emerges like a superb flower, amid the imitative verse-making of that middle period (common to all people) of life's mid-day. It links the brilliant young iconoclast of the early novels with the gentle character who was revealed after the intellectualistic dabbling with drugs, into a real serenity, as master of his fully defined perennial philosophy.

RICHARD CHURCH

I

The Burning Wheel

(1916)

The Burning Wheel was published as number seven in
Basil H. Blackwell's Oxford "Adventurers All" Series,
"A Series of Young Poets Unknown to Fame."

THE BURNING WHEEL

Wearied of its own turning,
Distressed with its own busy restlessness,
Yearning to draw the circumferent pain –
The rim that is dizzy with speed –
To the motionless centre, there to rest,
The wheel must strain through agony
On agony contracting, returning
Into the core of steel.
   And at last the wheel has rest, is still,
Shrunk to an adamant core:
Fulfilling its will in fixity.
But the yearning atoms, as they grind
Closer and closer, more and more
Fiercely together, beget
A flaming fire upward leaping,
Billowing out in a burning,
Passionate, fierce desire to find
The infinite calm of the mother's breast.
And there the flame is a Christ-child sleeping,
Bright, tenderly radiant;
All bitterness lost in the infinite
Peace of the mother's bosom.
But death comes creeping in a tide
Of slow oblivion, till the flame in fear
Wakes from the sleep of its quiet brightness
And burns with a darkening passion and pain,
Lest, all forgetting in quiet, it perish.
And as it burns and anguishes it quickens,
Begetting once again the wheel that yearns –
Sick with its speed – for the terrible stillness
Of the adamant core and the steel-hard chain.
And so once more
Shall the wheel revolve till its anguish cease

In the iron anguish of fixity;
Till once again
Flame billows out to infinity,
Sinking to a sleep of brightness
In that vast oblivious peace.

"The Burning Wheel" appears under the earlier title "The Wheel" in *The Palatine Review*, III (1916) and in the 1916 issue of *Oxford Poetry*.

DOORS OF THE TEMPLE

Many are the doors of the spirit that lead
    Into the inmost shrine:
And I count the gates of the temple divine,
    Since the god of the place is God indeed.
    And these are the gates that God decreed
Should lead to his house: – kisses and wine,
Cool depths of thought, youth without rest,
    And calm old age, prayer and desire,
The lover's and mother's breast,
    The fire of sense and the poet's fire.

But he that worships the gates alone,
    Forgetting the shrine beyond, shall see
    The great valves open suddenly,
Revealing, not God's radiant throne,
    But the fires of wrath and agony.

VILLIERS DE L'ISLE-ADAM

Up from the darkness on the laughing stage
A sudden trap-door shot you unawares,
Incarnate Tragedy, with your strange airs
Of courteous sadness. Nothing could assuage
The secular grief that was your heritage,

Passed down the long line to the last that bears
The name, a gift of yearnings and despairs
Too greatly noble for this iron age.

Time moved for you not in quotidian beats,
But in the long slow rhythm the ages keep
In their immortal symphony. You taught
That not in the harsh turmoil of the streets
Does life consist; you bade the soul drink deep
Of infinite things, saying: "The rest is naught."

DARKNESS

My close-walled soul has never known
That innermost darkness, dazzling sight,
Like the blind point, whence the visions spring
In the core of the gazer's chrysolite . . .
The mystic darkness that laps God's throne
In a splendour beyond imagining,
    So passing bright.

But the many twisted darknesses
That range the city to and fro,
In aimless subtlety pass and part
And ebb and glutinously flow;
Darkness of lust and avarice,
Of the crippled body and the crooked heart . . .
    These darknesses I know.

MOLE

Tunnelled in solid blackness creeps
The old mole-soul, and wakes or sleeps,
He knows not which, but tunnels on
Through ages of oblivion;

Until at last the long constraint
Of each-hand wall is lost, and faint
Comes daylight creeping from afar,
And mole-work grows crepuscular.
Tunnel meets air and bursts; mole sees
Men hugely walking ... or are they trees?
And far horizons smoking blue,
And chasing clouds for ever new;
Green hills, like lighted lamps aglow
Or quenching 'neath the cloud-shadow;
Quenching and blazing turn by turn,
Spring's great green signals fitfully burn.
Mole travels on, but finds the steering
A harder task of pioneering
Than when he thridded through the strait
Blind catacombs that ancient fate
Had carved for him. Stupid and dumb
And blind and touchless he had come
A way without a turn; but here,
Under the sky, the passenger
Chooses his own best way; and mole
Distracted wanders, yet his hole
Regrets not much wherein he crept,
But runs, a joyous nympholept,
This way and that, by all made mad –
River nymph and oread,
Ocean's daughters and Lorelei,
Combing the silken mystery,
The glaucous gold of her rivery tresses –
Each haunts the traveller, each possesses
The drunken wavering soul awhile;
Then with a phantom's cock-crow smile
Mocks craving with sheer vanishment.
  Mole-eyes grow hawk's; knowledge is [l]ent
In grudging driblets that pay high
Unconscionable usury
To unrelenting life. Mole learns
To travel more secure; the turns

Of his long way less puzzling seem,
And all those magic forms that gleam
In airy invitation cheat
Less often than they did of old.
　　The earth slopes upward, fold by fold
Of quiet hills that meet the gold
Serenity of western skies.
Over the world's edge with clear eyes
Our mole transcendent sees his way
Tunnelled in light: he must obey
Necessity again and third
Close catacombs as erst he did,
Fate's tunnellings himself must bore
Through the sunset's inmost core.
The guiding walls to each-hand shine
Luminous and crystalline;
And mole shall tunnel on and on,
Till night let fall oblivion.

THE TWO SEASONS

Summer, on himself intent,
　　Passed without, for nothing caring
　　Save his own high festival.
　My windows, blind and winkless staring,
Wondered what the pageant meant,
　　Nor ever understood at all.
And oh, the pains of sentiment!
　The loneliness beyond all bearing . . .
　　Mucus and spleen and gall!

But now that grey November peers
　In at my fire-bright window pane;
　　And all its misty spires and trees
　Loom in upon me through the rain
And question of the light that cheers
　　The room within – now my soul sees

Life, where of old were sepulchres;
    And in these new-found sympathies
Sinks petty hopes and loves and fears,
    And knows that life is not in vain.

TWO REALITIES

A waggon passed with scarlet wheels
    And a yellow body, shining new.
"Splendid!" said I. "How fine it feels
To be alive, when beauty peels
    The grimy husk from life." And you

Said, "Splendid!" and I thought you'd seen
    That waggon blazing down the street;
But I looked and saw that your gaze had been
On a child that was kicking an obscene
    Brown ordure with his feet.

Our souls are elephants, thought I,
    Remote behind a prisoning grill,
With trunks thrust out to peer and pry
And pounce upon reality;
    And each at his own sweet will

Seizes the bun that he likes best
And passes over all the rest.

QUOTIDIAN VISION

There is a sadness in the street,
And sullenly the folk I meet
Droop their heads as they walk along,
Without a smile, without a song.

A mist of cold and muffling grey
Falls, fold by fold, on another day
That dies unwept. But suddenly,
Under a tunnelled arch I see
On flank and haunch the chestnut gleam
Of horses in a lamplit steam;
And the dead world moves for me once more
With beauty for its living core.

VISION

I had been sitting alone with books,
    Till doubt was a black disease,
When I heard the cheerful shout of rooks
    In the bare, prophetic trees.

Bare trees, prophetic of new birth,
    You lift your branches clean and free
To be a beacon to the earth,
    A flame of wrath for all to see.

And the rooks in the branches laugh and shout
    To those that can hear and understand:
"Walk through the gloomy ways of doubt
    With the torch of vision in your hand."

THE MIRROR

Slow-moving moonlight once did pass
Across the dreaming looking-glass,
Where, sunk inviolably deep,
Old secrets unforgotten sleep
Of beauties unforgettable.

But dusty cobwebs are woven now
Across that mirror, which of old
Saw fingers drawing back the gold
From an untroubled brow;
And the depths are blinded to the moon,
And their secrets forgotten, for ever untold.

VARIATIONS ON A THEME OF LAFORGUE

Youth as it opens out discloses
The sinister metempsychosis
Of lilies dead and turned to roses
Red as an angry dawn.
But lilies, remember, are grave-side flowers,
    While slow bright rose-leaves sail
Adrift on the music of happiest hours;
    And those lilies, cold and pale,
Hide fiery roses beneath the lawn
    Of the young bride's parting veil.

PHILOCLEA IN THE FOREST

I

'Twas I that leaned to Amoret
With: "What if the briars have tangled Time,
Till, lost in the wood-ways, he quite forget
How plaintive in cities at midnight sounds the chime
Of bells slow-dying from discord to the hush whence
    they rose and met.

"And in the forest we shall live free,
Free from the bondage that Time has made
To hedge our soul from its liberty;

We shall not fear what is mighty, and unafraid
Shall look wide-eyed at beauty, nor shrink from its
    majesty."

But Amoret answered me again:
"We are lost in the forest, you and I;
Lost, lost, not free, though no bonds restrain;
For no spire rises for comfort, no landmark in the sky,
And the long glades as they curve from sight are dark
    with a nameless pain.

And Time creates what he devours, –
Music that sweetly dreams itself away,
Frail-swung leaves of autumn and the scent of flowers,
And the beauty of that poised moment, when the day
Hangs 'twixt the quiet of darkness and the mirth of
    the sunlit hours."

II

Mottled and grey and brown they pass,
The wood-moths, wheeling, fluttering;
And we chase and they vanish; and in the grass
Are starry flowers, and the birds sing
Faint broken songs of the dying spring.
    And on the beech-bole, smooth and grey,
    Some lover of an older day
Has carved in time-blurred lettering
    One word only: – "Alas."

III

Lutes, I forbid you! You must never play,
    When shimmeringly, glimpse by glimpse
Seen through the leaves, the silken figures sway
In measured dance. Never at shut of day,
    When Time perversely loitering limps

Through endless twilights, should your strings
   Whisper of light remembered things
That happened long ago and far away:
Lutes, I forbid you! You must never play . . .

And you, pale marble statues, far descried
   Where vistas open suddenly,
I bid you shew yourselves no more, but hide
Your loveliness, lest too much glorified
   By western radiance slantingly
   Shot down the glade, you turn from stone
   To living gods, immortal grown,
And, ageless, mock my beauty's fleeting pride,
You pale, relentless statues, far descried . . .

BOOKS AND THOUGHTS

Old ghosts that death forgot to ferry
Across the Lethe of the years –
These are my friends, and at their tears
I weep and with their mirth am merry.
On a high tower, whose battlements
Give me all heaven at a glance,
I lie long summer nights in trance,
Drowsed by the murmurs and the scents
That rise from earth, while the sky above me
Merges its peace with my soul's peace,
Deep meeting deep. No stir can move me,
Nought break the quiet of my release:
   In vain the windy sunlight raves
   At the hush and gloom of polar caves.

"CONTRARY TO NATURE AND ARISTOTLE"

One head of my soul's amphisbaena
Turns to the daytime's dust and sweat;
But evenings come, when I would forget
The sordid strife of the arena.

And then my other self will creep
Along the scented twilight lanes
To where a little house contains
A hoard of books, a gift of sleep.

Its windows throw a friendly light
Between the narrowing shutter slats,
And, golden as the eyes of cats,
Shine me a welcome through the night.

ESCAPE

I seek the quietude of stones
Or of great oxen, dewlap-deep
In meadows of lush grass, where sleep
Drifts, tufted, on the air or drones
On flowery traffic. Sleep atones
For sin, comforting eyes that weep.
O'er me, Lethean darkness, creep
Unfelt as tides through dead men's bones!

In that metallic sea of hair,
Fragrance! I come to drown despair
Of wings in dark forgetfulness.
No love ... Love is self-known, aspires
To heights unearthly. I ask less, –
Sleep born of satisfied desires.

THE GARDEN

There shall be dark trees round me: I insist
On cypresses: I'm terribly romantic –
And glimpsed between shall move the whole Atlantic,
Now leaden dull, now subtle with grey mist,
Now many jewelled, when the waves are kissed
By revelling sunlight and the corybantic
South-Western wind: so, troubled, passion-frantic,
The poet's mind boils gold and amethyst.

There shall be seen the infinite endeavor
Of a sad fountain, white against the sky
And poised as it strains up, but doomed to break
In weeping music; ever fair and ever
Young . . . and the bright-eyed wood-gods as they slake
Their thirst in it, are silent, reverently . . .

THE CANAL

No dip and dart of swallows wakes the black
Slumber of the canal: – a mirror dead
For lack of loveliness rememberéd
From ancient azures and green trees, for lack
Of some white beauty given and flung back,
Secret, to her that gave: no sun has bled
To wake an echo here of answering red;
The surface stirs to no leaf's wind-blown track.

Between unseeing walls the waters rest,
Lifeless and hushed, till suddenly a swan
Glides from some broader river blue as day,
And with the mirrored magic of his breast
Creates within that barren water-way
New life, new loveliness, and passes on.

THE IDEAL FOUND WANTING

I'm sick of clownery and Owlglass tricks;
Damn the whole crowd of you! I hate you all.
The same, night after night, from powdered stall
To sweating gallery, your faces fix
In flux an idiot mean. The Apteryx
You worship is no victory; you call
On old stupidity, God made to crawl
For tempting with world-wisdom's narcotics.

I'll break a window through my prison! See,
The sunset bleeds among the roofs; comes night,
Dark blue and calm as music dying out.
Is it escape? No, the laugh's turned on me!
I kicked at cardboard, gaped at red limelight;
You laughed and cheered my latest knockabout.

MISPLACED LOVE

Red wine that slowly leaned and brimmed the shell
Of pearl, where lips had touched, as light and swift
As naked petals of the rose adrift
Upon the lazy-luted ritournelle
Of summer bee-song: laughing as they fell,
Gold memories: dream incense, childhood's gift,
Blue as the smoke that far horizons lift,
Tenuous as the wings of Ariel: –

These treasured things I laid upon the pyre;
And the flame kindled, and I fanned it high,
And, strong in hope, could watch the crumbling past.
Eager I knelt before the waning fire,
Phoenix, to greet thine immortality . . .
But there was naught but ashes at the last.

SONNET

Were I to die, you'd break your heart, you say.
Well, if it do but bend, I'm satisfied –
Bend and rebound – for hearts are temper-tried,
Mild steel, not hardened, with the spring and play
Of excellent tough swords. It's not that way
That you'll be perishing. But when I've died,
When snap! my light goes out, what will betide
You, if the heart-breaks give you leave to stay?

What will be left, I wonder, if you lose
All that you gave me? "All? A year or so
Out of a life," you say. But worlds, say I,
Of kisses timeless given in ecstasy
That gave me Real You. I die: you go
With me. What's left? Limbs, clothes, a pair of shoes? . . .

SENTIMENTAL SUMMER

The West has plucked its flowers and has thrown
Them fading on the night. Out of the sky's
Black depths there smiles a greeting from those eyes,
Where all the Real, all I have ever known
Of the divine is held. And not alone
Do I stand here now . . . a presence seems to rise:
Your voice sounds near across my memories,
And answering fingers brush against my own.

Yes, it is you: for evening holds those strands
Of fire and darkness twined in one to make
Your loveliness a web of magic mesh,
Whose cross-weft harmony of soul and flesh
Shadows a thought or glows, when smiles awake,
Like sunlight passionate on southern lands.

THE CHOICE

Comrade, now that you're merry
And therefore true,
Say – where would you like to die
And have your friend to bury
What once was you?
"On the top of a hill
With a peaceful view
Of country where all is still?" . . .
Great God, not I!
I'd lie in thè street
Where two streams meet
And there's noise enough to fill
The outer ear,
While within the brain can beat
Marches of death and life,
Glory and joy and fear,
Peace of the sort that moves
And clash of strife
And routs of armies fleeing.
There would I shake myself clear
Out of the deep-set grooves
Of my sluggish being.

THE HIGHER SENSUALISM

There's a church by a lake in Italy
Stands white on a hill against the sky;
And a path of immemorial cobbles
Leads up and up, where the pilgrim hobbles
Past a score or so of neat reposories,
Where you stop and breathe and tell your rosaries
To the shrined terra-cotta mannikins,
That expound with the liveliest quirks and grins

Known texts of Scripture. But no long stay
Should the pilgrim make upon his way;
But as means to the end these shrines stand here
To guide to something holier,
The church on the hill-top.

                              Your heaven's so,
With a path leading up to it past a row
Of votary Priapulids;
At each you pause and tell your beads
Along the quintuple strings of sense:
Then on, to face Heaven's eminence,
New stimulated, new inspired.

SONNET

If that a sparkle of true starshine be
That led my way; if some diviner thing
Than common thought urged me to fashioning
Close-woven links of burnished poetry;
Then all the heaven that one time dwelt in me
Has fled, leaving the body triumphing.
Dead flesh it seems, with not a dream to bring
Visions that better warm immediacy.

Why have my visions left me, what could kill
That feeble spark, which yet had life and heat?
Fulfilment shewed a present rich and fair:
I strive to mount, but catch the nearest still:
Souls have been drowned between heart's beat and beat,
And trapped and tangled in a woman's hair.

FORMAL VERSES

I

Mother of all my future memories,
Mistress of my new life, which but to-day
Began, when I beheld, deep in your eyes,
My own love mirrored and the warm surprise
    Of the first kiss swept both our souls away,

Your love has freed me; for I was oppressed
    By my own devil, whose unwholesome breath
Tarnished my youth, leaving to me at best
Age lacking comfort of a soul at rest
    And weariness beyond the hope of death.

II

Ah, those were days of silent happiness!
    I never spoke, and had no need to speak,
    While on the windy down-land, cheek by cheek,
The slow-driven sun beheld us. Each caress
Had oratory for its own defence;
And when I kissed or felt her fingers press,
    I envied not Demosthenes his Greek,
Nor Tully for his Latin eloquence.

PERILS OF THE SMALL HOURS

When life burns low as the fire in the grate
And all the evening's books are read,
I sit alone, save for the dead
And the lovers I have grown to hate.

But all at once the narrow gloom
Of hatred and despair expands
In tenderness: thought stretches hands
To welcome to the midnight room

Another presence: – a memory
Of how last year in the sunlit field,
Laughing, you suddenly revealed
Beauty in immortality.

For so it is; a gesture strips
Life bare of all its make-believe.
All unprepared we may receive
Our casual apocalypse.

Sheer beauty, then you seemed to stir
Unbodied soul; soul sleeps to-night,
And love comes, dimming spirit's sight,
When body plays interpreter.

COMPLAINT

I have tried to remember the familiar places, –
    The pillared gloom of the beechwoods, the towns by the sea, –
I have tried to people the past with dear known faces,
    But you were haunting me.

Like a remorse, insistent, pitiless,
    You have filled my spirit, you were ever at hand;
You have mocked my gods with your new loveliness:
    Broken the old shrines stand.

RETURN TO AN OLD HOME

In this wood – how the hazels have grown! –
I left a treasure all my own
Of childish kisses and laughter and pain;
Left, till I might come back again
To take from the familiar earth
My hoarded secret and count its worth.
And all the spider-work of the years,
All the time-spun gossamers,
Dewed with each succeeding spring;
And the piled up leaves the Autumns fling
To the sweet corruption of death on death ...
At the sudden stir of my spirit's breath
All scattered. New and fair and bright
As ever it was, before my sight
The treasure lay, and nothing missed.
So having handled all and kissed,
I put them back, adding one new
And precious memory of you.

FRAGMENT

We're German scholars poring over life
As over a Greek manuscript that's torn
And stained beyond repair. Our eyes of horn
Read one or two poor letters; and what strife,
What books on books begotten for their sake!
But we enjoy it; and meanwhile neglect
The line that's left us perfect from the wrecked
Rich argosy, clear beyond doubts to make
Conjectures of. So in my universe
Of scribbled half-hid meanings you appear,
Sole perfect symbol of the highest sphere;
And life's great matrix crystal, whose depths nurse
Soul's infinite reflections, glows in you
With now uncertain radiance ...

THE WALK

I. Through the Suburbs

Provincial Sunday broods above the town:
The street's asleep; through a dim window drifts
A small romance that hiccoughs up and down
An air all trills and runs and sudden lifts
To yearning sevenths poised . . . not Chopin quite,
But, oh, romantic; a tinsel world made bright
With rose and honeysuckle's paper blooms,
And where the moon's blue limelight and the glooms
Of last-act scenes of passion are discreet.
And when the tinkling stops and leaves the street
Blank in the sunlight of the afternoon
You feel a curtain dropped. Poor little tune!
Perhaps our grandmother's dull girlhood days
Were fired by you with radiances of pink,
Heavenly, brighter far than she could think
Anything might be . . . till a greater blaze
Tinged life's horizon, when he kissed her first,
Our grandpapa. But a thin ghost still plays
In music down the street, echoing the plaint
Of far romance with its own sadder song
Of Everyday; and as they walk along, . . .
The young man and the woman, deep immersed
In all the suburb-comedy around . . .
They seem to catch coherence in the sound
Of that ghost-music, and the words come faint: –

> Oh the months and the days,
> Oh sleeps and dinners,
> Oh the planning of ways
> And quotidian means!
> Oh endless vistas of mutton and greens,
> Oh weekly mumblings of prayer and praise,
> Oh Evenings with All the Winners!
> Monday sends the clothes to wash
> And Saturday brings them home again:

Mon Dieu, la vie est par trop moche
And Destiny is a sale caboche;
    But I'll give you heaven
    In a dominant seven,
    And you shall not have lived in vain.
"In vain," the girl repeats, "in vain, in vain . . . "
Your suburb's whole philosophy leads there.
The ox-stall for our happiness, for pain,
Poignant and sweet, the dull narcotic ache
Of wretchedness, and in resigned despair
A grim contentment . . . ashen fruits to slake
A nameless, quenchless thirst. The tinkling rain
Of that small sentimental music wets
Your parching suburb: it may sprout . . . who knows? . . .
In something red and silken like a rose,
In sheaves of almost genuine violets.

Faint chords, your sadness, secular, immense,
Brims to the bursting this poor Actual heart.
For surging through the floodgates that the sense
On sudden lightly opens sweeps the Whole
Into the narrow compass of its part.

He

Inedited sensation of the soul!
You'd have us bless the Hire-Purchase System,
Which now allows the poorest vampers
To feel, as they abuse their piano's dampers,
That angels have stooped down and kissed 'em
With Ave-Maries from the infinite.
But poor old Infinite's dead. Long live his heir,
Lord Here-and-Now . . . for all the rest
Is windy nothingness, or at the best
Home-made Chimera, bodied with despair,
Headed with formless, foolish hope.

She

No, no!
We live in verse, for all things rhyme
With something out of space and time.

He

But in the suburb here life needs must flow
In journalistic prose . . .

She

But we have set
Our faces towards the further hills, where yet
The wind untainted and unbound may blow.

II. From the Crest

So through the squalor, till the sky unfolds
To right and left its fringes, penned no more,
A thin canal, 'twixt shore and ugly shore
Of hovels, poured contiguous from the moulds
Of Gothic horror. Town is left at last,
Save for the tentacles that probe, . . . a squat
Dun house or two, allotments, plot on plot
Of cabbage, jejeune, ripe or passed,
Chequering with sick yellow or verdigris
The necropolitan ground; and neat paved ways
That edge the road . . . the town's last nerves . . . and cease,
As if in sudden shame, where hedges raise
Their dusty greenery on either hand.
Their path mounts slowly up the hill;
And, as they walk, to right and left expand
The plain and the golden uplands and the blue
Faint smoke of distances that fade from view;
And at their feet, remote and still,
The city spreads itself.

He

That glabrous dome that lifts itself so grand,
There in the marish, is the omphalos,
The navel, umbo, middle, central boss
Of the unique, sole, true Cloud-Cuckoo Land.
Drowsy with Sunday bells and Sunday beer
Afoam in silver rumkins, there it basks,
Thinking of labours past and future tasks
And pondering on the end, forever near,
Yet ever distant as the rainbow's spring.
For still in Cuckoo-Land they're labouring,
With hopes undamped and undiscouraged hearts:
A little musty, but superb, they sit,
Piecing a god together bit by bit
Out of the chaos of his sundered parts.
Unmoved, nay pitying, they view the grins
And lewd grimaces of the folk that jeer . . .
The vulgar herd, gross monster at the best,
Obscenum Mobile, the uttermost sphere,
Alas, too much the mover of the rest,
Though they turn sungates to its widdershins . . .
And in some half a million years perhaps
God may at last be made . . . a new, true Pan,
An Isis templed in the soul of man,
An Aphrodite with her thousand paps
Streaming eternal wisdom.
Yes, and man's vessel, all pavilioned out
With silk and flags in the fair wind astream,
Shall make the port at last, with a great shout
Ringing from all her decks, and rocking there shall dream
For ever, and dream true . . . calm in those roads
As lovers' souls at evening, when they swim
Between the despairing sunset and the dim
Blue memories of mountains lost to sight
But, like half fancied, half remembered episodes
Of childhood, guessed at through the veils of night.
And the worn sailors at the mast who heard

37

The first far bells and knew the sound for home,
Who marked the land-weeds and the sand-stained foam
And through the storm-blast saw a wildered bird
Seek refuge at the mast-head ... these at last
Shall earn due praise when all the hubbub's past;
And Cuckoo-Landers not a few shall prove.

She

You have fast closed the temple gates;
    You stand without in the noon-tides glow,
But the innermost darkness, where God waits,
    You do not know, you cannot know.

2

The Defeat of Youth and Other Poems

(1918)

The Defeat of Youth was published as number three in
Basil H. Blackwell's Oxford "Initiates: a Series of Poetry
by Proved Hands".

THE DEFEAT OF YOUTH

I. Under the Trees

There had been phantoms, pale-remembered shapes
Of this and this occasion, sisterly
In their resemblances, each effigy
Crowned with the same bright hair above the nape's
White rounded firmness, and each body alert
With such swift loveliness, that very rest
Seemed a poised movement: . . . phantoms that impressed
But a faint influence and could bless or hurt
No more than dreams. And these ghost things were she;
For formless still, without identity,
Not one she seemed, not clear, but many and dim.
One face among the legions of the street,
Indifferent mystery, she was for him
Something still uncreated, incomplete.

II

Bright windy sunshine and the shadow of cloud
Quicken the heavy summer to new birth
Of life and motion on the drowsing earth;
The huge elms stir, till all the air is loud
With their awakening from the muffled sleep
Of long hot days. And on the wavering line
That marks the alternate ebb of shade and shine,
Under the trees, a little group is deep
In laughing talk. The shadow as it flows
Across them dims the lustre of a rose,
Quenches the bright clear gold of hair, the green
Of a girl's dress, and life seems faint. The light
Swings back, and in the rose a fire is seen,
Gold hair's aflame and green grows emerald bright.

III

She leans, and there is laughter in the face
She turns towards him; and it seems a door
Suddenly opened on some desolate place
With a burst of light and music. What before
Was hidden shines in loveliness revealed.
Now first he sees her beautiful, and knows
That he must love her; and the doom is sealed
Of all his happiness and all the woes
That shall be born of pregnant years hereafter.
The swift poise of a head, a flutter of laughter –
And love flows in on him, its vastness pent
Within his narrow life: the pain it brings,
Boundless; for love is infinite discontent
With the poor lonely life of transient things.

IV

Men see their god, an immanence divine,
Smile through the curve of flesh or moulded clay,
In bare ploughed lands that go sloping away
To meet the sky in one clean exquisite line.
Out of the short-seen dawns of ecstasy
They draw new beauty, whence new thoughts are born
And in their turn conceive, as grains of corn
Germ and create new life and endlessly
Shall live creating. Out of earthly seeds
Springs the aerial flower. One spirit proceeds
Through change, the same in body and in soul –
The spirit of life and love that triumphs still
In its slow struggle towards some far-off goal
Through lust and death and the bitterness of will.

V

One spirit it is that stirs the fathomless deep
Of human minds, that shakes the elms in storm,

42

That sings in passionate music, or on warm
Still evenings bosoms forth the tufted sleep
Of thistle-seeds that wait a travelling wind.
One spirit shapes the subtle rhythms of thought
And the long thundering seas; the soul is wrought
Of one stuff with the body – matter and mind
Woven together in so close a mesh
That flowers may blossom into a song, that flesh
May strangely teach the loveliest holiest things
To watching spirits. Truth is brought to birth
Not in some vacant heaven: its beauty springs
From the dear bosom of material earth.

VI. In the Hayloft

The darkness in the loft is sweet and warm
With the stored hay . . . darkness intensified
By one bright shaft that enters through the wide
Tall doors from under fringes of a storm
Which makes the doomed sun brighter. On the hay,
Perched mountain-high they sit, and silently
Watch the motes dance and look at the dark sky
And mark how heartbreakingly far away
And yet how close and clear the distance seems,
While all at hand is cloud – brightness of dreams
Unrealisable, yet seen so clear,
So only just beyond the dark. They wait,
Scarce knowing what they wait for, half in fear;
Expectance draws the curtain from their fate.

VII

The silence of the storm weighs heavily
On their strained spirits: sometimes one will say
Some trivial thing as though to ward away
Mysterious powers, that imminently lie
In wait, with the strong exorcising grace
Of everyday's futility. Desire

Becomes upon a sudden a crystal fire,
Defined and hard: – If he could kiss her face,
Could kiss her hair! As if by chance, her hand
Brushes on his . . . Ah, can she understand?
Or is she pedestalled above the touch
Of his desire? He wonders: dare he seek
From her that little, that infinitely much?
And suddenly she kissed him on the cheek.

VIII. Mountains

A stronger gust catches the cloud and twists
A spindle of rifted darkness through its heart,
A gash in the damp grey, which, thrust apart,
Reveals black depths a moment. Then the mists
Shut down again: a white uneasy sea
Heaves round the climbers and beneath their feet.
He strains on upwards through the wind and sleet,
Poised, or swift moving, or laboriously
Lifting his weight. And if he should let go,
What would he find down there, down there below
The curtain of the mist? What would he find
Beyond the dim and stifling now and here,
Beneath the unsettled turmoil of his mind?
Oh, there were nameless depths: he shrank with fear.

IX

The hills more glorious in their coat of snow
Rise all around him, in the valleys run
Bright streams, and there are lakes that catch the sun,
And sunlit fields of emerald far below
That seem alive with inward light. In smoke
The far horizons fade; and there is peace
On everything, a sense of blessed release
From wilful strife. Like some prophetic cloak
The spirit of the mountains has descended
On all the world, and its unrest is ended.

Even the sea, glimpsed far away, seems still,
Hushed to a silver peace its storm and strife.
Mountains of vision, calm above fate and will,
You hold the promise of the freer life.

X. In the Little Room

London unfurls its incense-coloured dusk
Before the panes, rich but a while ago
With the charred gold and the red ember-glow
Of dying sunset. Houses quit the husk
Of secrecy, which, through the day, returns
A blank to all enquiry: but at nights
The cheerfulness of fire and lamp invites
The darkness inward, curious of what burns
With such a coloured life when all is dead –
The daylight world outside, with overhead
White clouds, and where we walk, the blaze
Of wet and sunlit streets, shops and the stream
Of glittering traffic – all that the nights erase,
Colour and speed, surviving but in dream.

XI

Outside the dusk, but in the little room
All is alive with light, which brightly glints
On curving cup or the stiff folds of chintz,
Evoking its own whiteness. Shadows loom,
Bulging and black, upon the walls, where hang
Rich coloured plates of beauties that appeal
Less to the sense of sight than to the feel,
So moistly satin are their breasts. A pang,
Almost of pain, runs through him when he sees
Hanging, a homeless marvel, next to these,
The silken breastplate of a mandarin,
Centuries dead, which he had given her.
Exquisite miracle, when men could spin
Jay's wing and belly of the kingfisher!

XII

In silence and as though expectantly
She crouches at his feet, while he caresses
His light-drawn fingers with the touch of tresses
Sleeked round her head, close-banded lustrously,
Save where at nape and temple the smooth brown
Sleaves out into a pale transparent mist
Of hair and tangled light. So to exist,
Poised 'twixt the deep of thought where spirits drown
Life in a void impalpable nothingness,
And, on the other side, the pain and stress
Of clamorous action and the gnawing fire
Of will, focal upon a point of earth – even thus
To sit, eternally without desire
And yet self-known, were happiness for us.

XIII

She turns her head and in a flash of laughter
Looks up at him: and helplessly he feels
That life has circled with returning wheels
Back to a starting-point. Before and after
Merge in this instant, momently the same:
For it was thus she leaned and laughing turned
When, manifest, the spirit of beauty burned
In her young body with an inward flame,
And first he knew and loved her. In full tide
Life halts within him, suddenly stupefied.
Sight blackness, lightning-struck; but blindly tender
He draws her up to meet him, and she lies
Close folded by his arms in glad surrender,
Smiling, and with drooped head and half-closed eyes.

XIV

"I give you all; would that I might give more."
He sees the colour dawn across her cheeks
And die again to white; marks as she speaks

The trembling of her lips, as though she bore
Some sudden pain and hardly mastered it.
Within his arms he feels her shuddering,
Piteously trembling like some wild wood-thing
Caught unawares. Compassion infinite
Mounts up within him. Thus to hold and keep
And comfort her distressed, lull her to sleep
And gently kiss her brow and hair and eyes
Seem love perfected – templed high and white
Against the calm of golden autumn skies,
And shining quenchlessly with vestal light.

XV

But passion ambushed by the aerial shrine
Comes forth to dance, a hoofed obscenity,
His satyr's dance, with laughter in his eye,
And cruelty along the scarlet line
Of his bright smiling mouth. All uncontrolled,
Love's rebel servant, he delights to beat
The maddening quick dry rhythm of goatish feet
Even in the sanctuary, and makes bold
To mime himself the godhead of the place.
He turns in terror from her trance-calmed face,
From the white-lidded languor of her eyes,
From lips that passion never shook before,
But glad in the promise of her sacrifice:
"I give you all; would that I might give more."

XVI

He is afraid, seeing her lie so still,
So utterly his own; afraid lest she
Should open wide her eyes and let him see
The passionate conquest of her virgin will
Shine there in triumph, starry-bright with tears.
He thrusts her from him: face and hair and breast,
Hands he had touched, lips that his lips had pressed,

47

Seem things deadly to be desired. He fears
Lest she should body forth in palpable shame
Those dreams and longings that his blood, aflamè
Through the hot dark of summer nights, had dreamed
And longed. Must all his love, then, turn to this?
Was lust the end of what so pure had seemed?
He must escape, ah God! her touch, her kiss.

XVII. In the Park

Laughing, "To-night," I said to him, "the Park
Has turned the garden of a symbolist.
Those old great trees that rise above the mist,
Gold with the light of evening, and the dark
Still water, where the dying sun evokes
An echoed glory – here I recognize
Those ancient gardens mirrored by the eyes
Of poets that hate the world of common folks,
Like you and me and that thin pious crowd,
Which yonder sings its hymns, so humbly proud
Of holiness. The garden of escape
Lies here; a small green world, and still the bride
Of quietness, although an imminent rape
Roars ceaselessly about on every side."

XVIII

I had forgotten what I had lightly said,
And without speech, without a thought I went,
Steeped in that golden quiet, all content
To drink the transient beauty as it sped
Out of eternal darkness into time
To light and burn and know itself a fire;
Yet doomed – ah, fate of the fulfilled desire !–
To fade, a meteor, paying for the crime
Of living glorious in the denser air
Of our material earth. A strange despair,

48

An agony, yet strangely, subtly sweet
And tender as an unpassionate caress,
Filled me . . . Oh laughter! youth's conceit
Grown almost conscious of youth's feebleness!

XIX

He spoke abrupt across my dream: "Dear Garden,
A stranger to your magic peace, I stand
Beyond your walls, lost in a fevered land
Of stones and fire. Would that the gods would harden
My soul against its torment, or would blind
Those yearning glimpses of a life at rest
In perfect beauty – glimpses at the best
Through unpassed bars. And here, without, the wind
Of scattering passion blows: and women pass
Glitter-eyed down putrid alleys where the glass
Of some grimed window suddenly parades –
Ah, sickening heart-beat of desire! – the grace
Of bare and milk-warm flesh: the vision fades,
And at the pane shows a blind tortured face."

XX. Self-Torment

The days pass by, empty of thought and will:
His thought grows stagnant at its very springs,
With every channel on the world of things
Dammed up, and thus, by its long standing still,
Poisons itself and sickens to decay.
All his high love for her, his fair desire,
Loses its light; and a dull rancorous fire,
Burning darkness and bitterness that prey
Upon his heart are left. His spirit burns
Sometimes with hatred, or the hatred turns
To a fierce lust for her, more cruel than hate,
Till he is weary wrestling with its force:
And evermore she haunts him, early and late,
As pitilessly as an old remorse.

49

XXI

Streets and the solitude of country places
Were once his friends. But as a man born blind,
Opening his eyes from lovely dreams, might find
The world a desert and men's larval faces
So hateful, he would wish to seek again
The darkness and his old chimeric sight
Of beauties inward – so, that fresh delight,
Vision of bright fields and angelic men,
That love which made him all the world, is gone.
Hating and hated now, he stands alone,
An island-point, measureless gulfs apart
From other lives, from the old happiness
Of being more than self, when heart to heart
Gave all, yet grew the greater, not the less.

XXII. The Quarry in the Wood

Swiftly deliberate, he seeks the place.
A small wind stirs, the copse is bright in the sun:
Like quicksilver the shine and shadow run
Across the leaves. A bramble whips his face,
The tears spring fast, and through the rainbow mist
He sees a world that wavers like the flame
Of a blown candle. Tears of pain and shame,
And lips that once had laughed and sung and kissed
Trembling in the passion of his sobbing breath!
The world a candle shuddering to its death,
And life a darkness, blind and utterly void
Of any love or goodness: all deceit,
This friendship and this God: all shams destroyed,
And truth seen now.
                        Earth fails beneath his feet.

SONG OF POPLARS

Shepherd, to yon tall poplars tune your flute:
Let them pierce, keenly, subtly shrill,
The slow blue rumour of the hill;
Let the grass cry with an anguish of evening gold,
And the great sky be mute.

Then hearken how the poplar trees unfold
Their buds, yet close and gummed and blind,
In airy leafage of the mind,
Rustling in silvery whispers the twin-hued scales
That fade not nor grow old.

"Poplars and fountains and you cypress spires
Springing in dark and rusty flame,
Seek you aught that hath a name?
Or say, say: Are you all an upward agony
Of undefined desires?

"Say, are you happy in the golden march
Of sunlight all across the day?
Or do you watch the uncertain way
That leads the withering moon on cloudy stairs
Over the heaven's wide arch?

"Is it towards sorrow or towards joy you lift
The sharpness of your trembling spears?
Or do you seek, through the grey tears
That blur the sky, in the heart of the triumphing blue,
A deeper, calmer rift?"

So; I have tuned my music to the trees,
And there were voices, dim below
Their shrillness, voices swelling slow
In the blue murmur of hills, and a golden cry
And then vast silences.

THE REEF

My green aquarium of phantom fish,
Goggling in on me through the misty panes;
My rotting leaves and fields spongy with rains;
My few clear quiet autumn days – I wish

I could leave all, clearness and mistiness;
Sodden or goldenly crystal, all too still.
Yes, and I too rot with the leaves that fill
The hollows in the woods; I am grown less

Than human, listless, aimless as the green
Idiot fishes of my aquarium,
Who loiter down their dim tunnels and come
And look at me and drift away, nought seen

Or understood, but only glazedly
Reflected. Upwards, upwards through the shadows,
Through the lush sponginess of deep-sea meadows
Where hare-lipped monsters batten, let me ply

Winged fins, bursting this matrix dark to find
Jewels and movement, mintage of sunlight
Scattered largely by the profuse wind,
And gulfs of blue brightness, too deep for sight.

Free, newly born, on roads of music and air
Speeding and singing, I shall seek the place
Where all the shining threads of water race,
Drawn in green ropes and foamy meshes. There,

On the red fretted ramparts of a tower
Of coral rooted in the depths, shall break
An endless sequence of joy and speed and power:
Green shall shatter to foam; flake with white flake

Shall create an instant's shining constellation
Upon the blue; and all the air shall be
Full of a million wings that swift and free
Laugh in the sun, all power and strong elation.

Yes, I shall seek that reef, which is beyond
All isles however magically sleeping
In tideless seas, uncharted and unconned
Save by blind eyes; beyond the laughter and weeping

That brood like a cloud over the lands of men.
Movement, passion of colour and pure wings,
Curving to cut like knives – these are the things
I search for: – passion beyond the ken

Of our foiled violences, and, more swift
Than any blow which man aims against time,
The invulnerable, motion that shall rift
All dimness with the lightning of a rhyme,

Or note, or colour. And the body shall be
Quick as the mind; and will shall find release
From bondage to brute things; and joyously
Soul, will and body, in the strength of triune peace,

Shall live the perfect grace of power unwasted.
And love consummate, marvellously blending
Passion and reverence in a single spring
Of quickening force, till now never yet tasted,

But ever ceaselessly thirsted for, shall crown
The new life with its ageless starry fire.
I go to seek that reef, far down, far down
Below the edge of everyday's desire,

Beyond the magical islands, where of old
I was content, dreaming, to give the lie
To misery. They were all strong and bold
That thither came; and shall I dare to try?

WINTER DREAM

Oh wind-swept towers,
Oh endlessly blossoming trees,
White clouds and lucid eyes,
And pools in the rocks whose unplumbed blue is pregnant
With who knows what of subtlety
And magical curves and limbs –
White Anadyomene and her shallow breasts
Mother-of-pearled with light.

And oh the April, April of straight soft hair,
Falling smooth as the mountain water and brown;
The April of little leaves unblinded,
Of rosy nipples and innocence
And the blue languor of weary eyelids.

Across a huge gulf I fling my voice
And my desires together:
Across a huge gulf . . . on the other bank
Crouches April with her hair as smooth and straight and brown
As falling waters.
Oh brave curve upwards and outwards.
Oh despair of the downward tilting –
Despair still beautiful
As a great star one has watched all night
Wheeling down under the hills.
Silence widens and darkens;
Voice and desires have dropped out of sight.
I am all alone, dreaming she would come and kiss me.

THE FLOWERS

Day after day,
At spring's return,
I watch my flowers, how they burn
Their lives away.

The candle crocus
And daffodil gold
Drink fire of the sunshine –
Quickly cold.

And the proud tulip –
How red he glows! –
Is quenched ere summer
Can kindle the rose.

Purple as the innermost
Core of a sinking flame,
Deep in the leaves the violets smoulder
To the dust whence they came.

Day after day
At spring's return
I watch my flowers, how they burn
Their lives away,
Day after day . . .

THE ELMS

Fine as the dust of plumy fountains blowing
Across the lanterns of a revelling night,
The tiny leaves of April's earliest growing
Powder the trees – so vaporously light,
They seem to float, billows of emerald foam
Blown by the South on its bright airy tide,
Seeming less trees than things beatified,
Come from the world of thought which was their home.

For a while only. Rooted strong and fast,
Soon will they lift towards the summer sky
Their mountain-mass of clotted greenery.
Their immaterial season quickly past,
They grow opaque, and therefore needs must die,
Since every earth to earth returns at last.

OUT OF THE WINDOW

In the middle of countries, far from hills and sea,
Are the little places one passes by in trains
And never stops at; where the skies extend
Uninterrupted, and the level plains
Stretch green and yellow and green without an end.
And behind the glass of their Grand Express
Folk yawn away a province through,
With nothing to think of, nothing to do,
Nothing even to look at – never a "view"
In this damned wilderness.
But I look out of the window and find
Much to satisfy the mind.
Mark how the furrows, formed and wheeled
In a motion orderly and staid,
Sweep, as we pass, across the field
Like a drilled army on parade.
And here's a market-garden, barred
With stripe on stripe of varied greens . . .
Bright potatoes, flower starred,
And the opacous colour of beans.
Each line deliberately swings
Towards me, till I see a straight
Green avenue to the heart of things,
The glimpse of a sudden opened gate
Piercing the adverse walls of fate . . .
A moment only, and then, fast, fast,
The gate swings to, the avenue closes;
Fate laughs and once more interposes
Its barriers.

                    The train has passed.

INSPIRATION

Noonday upon the Alpine meadows
Pours its avalanche of Light
And blazing flowers: the very shadows
Translucent are and bright.
It seems a glory that nought surpasses –
Passion of angels in form and hue –
When, lo! from the jewelled heaven of the grasses
Leaps a lightning of sudden blue.
Dimming the sun-drunk petals,
Bright even unto pain,
The grasshopper flashes, settles,
And then is quenched again.

SUMMER STILLNESS

The stars are golden instants in the deep
Flawless expanse of night: the moon is set:
The river sleeps, entranced, a smooth cool sleep
Seeming so motionless that I forget
The hollow booming bridges, where it slides,
Dark with the sad looks that it bears along,
Towards a sea whose unreturning tides
Ravish the sighted ships and the sailors' song.

ANNIVERSARIES

Once more the windless days are here,
Quiet of autumn, when the year
Halts and looks backward and draws breath
Before it plunges into death.
Silver of mist and gossamers,

Through-shine of noonday's glassy gold,
Pale blue of skies, where nothing stirs
Save one blanched leaf, weary and old,
That over and over slowly falls
From the mute elm-trees, hanging on air
Like tattered flags along the walls
Of chapels deep in sunlit prayer.
Once more ... Within its flawless glass
To-day reflects that other day,
When, under the bracken, on the grass,
We who were lovers happily lay
And hardly spoke, or framed a thought
That was not one with the calm hills
And crystal sky. Ourselves were nought,
Our gusty passions, our burning wills
Dissolved in boundlessness, and we
Were almost bodiless, almost free.

The wind has shattered silver and gold.
Night after night of sparkling cold,
Orion lifts his tangled feet
From where the tossing branches beat
In a fine surf against the sky.
So the trance ended, and we grew
Restless, we know not how or why;
And there were sudden gusts that blew
Our dreaming banners into storm;
We wore the uncertain crumbling form
Of a brown swirl of windy leaves,
A phantom shape that stirs and heaves
Shuddering from earth, to fall again
With a dry whisper of withered rain.

Last, from the dead and shrunken days
We conjured spring, lighting the blaze
Of burnished tulips in the dark;
And from black frost we struck a spark
Of blue delight and fragrance new,
A little world of flowers and dew.

Winter for us was over and done:
The drought of fluttering leaves had grown
Emerald shining in the sun,
As light as glass, as firm as stone.
Real once more: for we had passed
Through passion into thought again;
Shaped our desires and made that fast
Which was before a cloudy pain;
Moulded the dimness, fixed, defined
In a fair statue, strong and free,
Twin bodies flaming into mind,
Poised on the brink of ecstasy.

ITALY

There is a country in my mind,
Lovelier than a poet blind
Could dream of, who had never known
This world of drought and dust and stone
In all its ugliness: a place
Full of an all but human grace;
Whose dells retain the printed form
Of heavenly sleep, and seem yet warm
From some pure body newly risen;
Where matter is no more a prison,
But freedom for the soul to know
Its native beauty. For things glow
There with an inward truth and are
All fire and colour like a star.
And in that land are domes and towers
That hang as light and bright as flowers
Upon the sky, and seem a birth
Rather of air than solid earth.

Sometimes I dream that walking there
In the green shade, all unaware
At a new turn of the golden glade,
I shall see her, and as though afraid
Shall halt a moment and almost fall
For passing faintness, like a man
Who feels the sudden spirit of Pan
Brimming his narrow soul with all
The illimitable world. And she,
Turning her head, will let me see
The first sharp dawn of her surprise
Turning to welcome in her eyes.
And I shall come and take my lover
And looking on her re-discover
All her beauty: – her dark hair
And the little ears beneath it, where
Roses of lucid shadow sleep;
Her brooding mouth, and in the deep
Wells of her eyes reflected stars . . .

Oh, the imperishable things
That hands and lips as well as words
Shall speak! Oh movement of white wings,
Oh wheeling galaxies of birds . . . !

THE ALIEN

A petal drifted loose
From a great magnolia bloom,
Your face hung in the gloom,
Floating, white and close.

We seemed alone: but another
Bent o'er you with lips of flame,
Unknown, without a name,
Hated, and yet my brother.

Your one short moan of pain
Was an exorcising spell:
The devil flew back to hell;
We were alone again.

WAKING

Darkness had stretched its colour,
Deep blue across the pane:
No cloud to make night duller,
No moon with its tarnish stain;
But only here and there a star,
One sharp point of frosty fire,
Hanging infinitely far
In mockery of our life and death
And all our small desire.

Now in this hour of waking
From under brows of stone,
A new pale day is breaking
And the deep night is gone.
Sordid now, and mean and small
The daylight world is seen again,
With only the veils of mist that fall
Deaf and muffling over all
To hide its ugliness and pain.

But to-day this dawn of meanness
Shines in my eyes, as when
The new world's brightness and cleanness
Broke on the first of men.
For the light that shows the huddled things
Of this close-pressing earth,
Shines also on your face and brings
All its dear beauty back to me
In a new miracle of birth.

I see you asleep and unpassioned,
White-faced in the dusk of your hair –
Your beauty so fleetingly fashioned
That it filled me once with despair
To look on its exquisite transience
And think that our love and thought and laughter
Puff out with the death of our flickering sense,
While we pass ever on and away
Towards some blank hereafter.

But now I am happy, knowing
That swift time is our friend,
And that our love's passionate glowing,
Though it turn ash in the end,
Is a rose of fire that must blossom its way
Through temporal stuff, nor else could be
More than a nothing. Into day
The boundless spaces of night contract
And in your opening eyes I see
Night born in day, in time eternity.

BY THE FIRE

We who are lovers sit by the fire,
Cradled warm 'twixt thought and will,
Sit and drowse like sleeping dogs
In the equipoise of all desire,
Sit and listen to the still
Small hiss and whisper of green logs
That burn away, that burn away
With the sound of a far-off falling stream
Of threaded water blown to steam,
Grey ghost in the mountain world of grey.
Vapours blue as distance rise
Between the hissing logs that show
A glimpse of rosy heat below;

And candles watch with tireless eyes
While we sit drowsing here. I know,
Dimly, that there exists a world,
That there is time perhaps, and space
Other and wider than this place,
Where at the fireside drowsily curled
We hear the whisper and watch the flame
Burn blinkless and inscrutable.
And then I know those other names
That through my brain from cell to cell
Echo – reverberated shout
Of waiters mournful along corridors:
But nobody carries the orders out,
And the names (dear friends, your name and yours)
Evoke no sign. But here I sit
On the wide hearth, and there are you:
That is enough and only true.
The world and the friends that lived in it
Are shadows: you alone remain
Real in this drowsing room,
Full of the whispers of distant rain
And candles staring into the gloom.

VALEDICTORY

I had remarked – how sharply one observes
When life is disappearing round the curves
Of yet another corner, out of sight! –
I had remarked when it was "good luck" and "good night"
And "a good journey to you", on her face
Certain enigmas penned in the hieroglyphs
Of that half frown and queer fixed smile and trace
Of clouded thought in those brown eyes,
Always so happily clear of hows and ifs –
My poor bleared mind! – and haunting whys.

There I stood, holding her farewell hand,
(Pressing my life and soul and all
The world to one good-bye, till, small
And smaller pressed, why there I'd stand
Dead when they vanished with thè sight of her).
And I saw that she had grown aware,
Queer puzzled face! of other things
Beyond the present and her own young speed,
Of yesterday and what new days might breed
Monstrously when the future brings
A charger with your late-lamented head:
Aware of other people's lives and will,
Aware, perhaps, aware even of me . . .
The joyous hope of it! But still
I pitied her; for it was sad to see
A goddess shorn of her divinity.
In the midst of her speed she had made pause,
And doubts with all their threat of claws,
Outstripped till now by her unconsciousness,
Had seized on her; she was proved mortal now.
"Live, only live! For you were meant
Never to know a thought's distress,
But a long glad astonishment
At the world's beauty and your own.
The pity of you, goddess, grown
Perplexed and mortal!"
                              Yet . . . yet . . . can it be
That she is aware, perhaps, even of me?

And life recedes, recedes; the curve is bare,
My handkerchief flutters blankly in the air;
And the question rumbles in the void:
Was she aware, was she after all aware?

LOVE SONG

Dear absurd child – too dear to my cost I've found –
God made your soul for pleasure, not for use:
It cleaves no way, but angled broad obtuse,
Impinges with a slabby-bellied sound
Full upon life, and on the rind of things
Rubs its sleek self and utters purr and snore
And all the gamut of satisfied murmurings,
Content with that, nor wishes anything more.

A happy infant, daubed to the eyes in juice
Of peaches that flush bloody at the core,
Naked you bask upon a south-sea shore,
While o'er your tumbling bosom the hair floats loose.
The wild flowers bloom and die; the heavens go round
With the song of wheeling planetary rings:
You wriggle in the sun; each moment brings
Its freight for you; in all things pleasures abound.

You taste and smile, then this for the next pass over;
And there's no future for you and no past,
And when, absurdly, death arrives at last,
'Twill please you awhile to kiss your latest lover.

PRIVATE PROPERTY

All fly – yet who is misanthrope? –
The actual men and things that pass
Jostling, to wither as the grass
So soon: and (be it heaven's hope,
Or poetry's kaleidoscope,
Or love or wine, at feast, at mass)
Each owns a paradise of glass
Where never a yearning heliotrope
Pursues the sun's ascent or slope;
For the sun dreams there, and no time is or was.

Like fauns embossed in our domain,
We look abroad, and our calm eyes
Mark how the goatish gods of pain
Revel; and if by grim surprise
They break into our paradise,
Patient we build its beauty up again.

REVELATION

At your mouth, white and milk-warm sphinx,
I taste a strange apocalypse:
Your subtle taper finger-tips
Weave me new heavens, yet, methinks,
I know the wiles and each iynx
That brought me passionate to your lips:
I know you bare as laughter strips
Your charnel beauty; yet my spirit drinks

Pure knowledge from this tainted well,
And now hears voices yet unheard
Within it, and without it sees
That world of which the poets tell
Their vision in the stammered word
Of those that wake from piercing ecstasies.

MINOAN PORCELAIN

Her eyes of bright unwinking glaze
All imperturbable do not
Even make pretences to regard
The jutting absence of her stays,
Where many a Tyrian gallipot
Excites desire with spilth of nard.

The bistered rims above the fard
Of cheeks as red as bergamot
Attest that no shamefaced delays
Will clog fulfilment, nor retard
Full payment of the Cyprian's praise
Down to the last remorseful jot.
Hail, priestess of we know not what
Strange cult of Mycenean days!

THE DECAMERON

Noon with a depth of shadow beneath the trees
Shakes in the heat, quivers to the sound of lutes:
Half shaded, half sunlit, a great bowl of fruits
Glistens purple and golden: the flasks of wine
Cool in their panniers of snow: silks muffle and shine:
Dim velvet, where through the leaves a sunbeam shoots,
Rifts in a pane of scarlet: fingers tapping the roots
Keep languid time to the music's soft slow decline.

Suddenly from the gate rises up a cry,
Hideous broken laughter, scarce human in sound;
Gaunt clawed hands, thrust through the bars despairingly,
Clutch fast at the scented air, while on the ground
Lie the poor plague-stricken carrions, who have found
Strength to crawl forth and curse the sunshine and die.

IN UNCERTAINTY TO A LADY

I am not one of those who sip,
Like a quotidian bock,
Cheap idylls from a languid lip
Prepared to yawn or mock.

I wait the indubitable word,
The great Unconscious Cue.
Has it been spoken and unheard?
Spoken, perhaps, by you ... ?

CRAPULOUS IMPRESSION

(To J.S.)

Still life, still life ... the high-lights shine
Hard and sharp on the bottles: the wine
Stands firmly solid in the glasses,
Smooth yellow ice, through which there passes
The lamp's bright pencil of down-struck light.
The fruits metallically gleam,
Globey in their heaped-up bowl,
And there are faces against the night
Of the outer room – faces that seem
Part of this still, still life ... they've lost their soul.

And amongst these frozen faces you smiled,
Surprised, surprisingly, like a child:
And out of the frozen welter of sound
Your voice came quietly, quietly.
"What about God?" you said. "I have found
Much to be said for Totality.
All, I take it, is God: God's all –
This bottle, for instance ... " I recall,
Dimly, that you took God by the neck –
God-in-the-bottle – and pushed Him across:
But I, without a moment's loss
Moved God-in-the-salt in front and shouted: "Check!"

THE LIFE THEORETIC

While I have been fumbling over books
And thinking about God and the Devil and all,
Other young men have been battling with the days
And others have been kissing the beautiful women.
They have brazen faces like battering-rams.
But I who think about books and such –
I crumble to impotent dust before the struggling,
And the women palsy me with fear.
But when it comes to fumbling over books
And thinking about God and the Devil and all,
Why, there I am.
But perhaps the battering-rams are in the right of it,
Perhaps, perhaps . . . God knows.

COMPLAINT OF A POET MANQUÉ

We judge by appearance merely:
If I can't think strangely, I can at least look queerly.
So I grew the hair so long on my head
That my mother wouldn't know me,
Till a woman in a night-club said,
As I was passing by,
"Hullo, here comes Salome . . . "

I looked in the dirty gilt-edged glass,
And, oh Salome! there I was –
Positively jewelled, half a vampire,
With the soul in my eyes hanging dizzily
Like the gatherer of proverbial samphire
Over the brink of the crag of sense,
Looking down from perilous eminence
Into a gulf of windy night.
And there's straw in my tempestuous hair,
And I'm not a poet: but never despair!
I'll madly live the poems I shall never write.

SOCIAL AMENITIES

I am getting on well with this anecdote,
When suddenly I recall
The many times I have told it of old,
And all the worked-up phrases, and the dying fall
Of voice, well timed in the crisis, the note
Of mock-heroic ingeniously struck –
The whole thing sticks in my throat,
And my face all tingles and pricks with shame
For myself and my hearers.
These are the social pleasures, my God!
But I finish the story triumphantly all the same.

TOPIARY

Failing sometimes to understand
Why there are folk whose flesh should seem
Like carrion puffed with noisome steam,
Fly-blown to the eye that looks on it,
Fly-blown to the touch of a hand;
Why there are men without any legs,
Whizzing along on little trollies
With long long arms like apes':
Failing to see why God the Topiarist
Should train and carve and twist
Men's bodies into such fantastic shapes:
Yes, failing to see the point of it all, I sometimes wish
That I were a fabulous thing in a fool's mind,
Or, at the ocean bottom, in a world that is deaf and blind,
Very remote and happy, a great goggling fish.

ON THE 'BUS

Sitting on the top of the 'bus,
I bite my pipe and look at the sky.
Over my shoulder the smoke streams out
And my life with it.
"Conservation of energy," you say.
But I burn, I tell you, I burn;
And the smoke of me streams out
In a vanishing skein of grey.
Crash and bump . . . my poor bruised body!
I am a harp of twittering strings,
An elegant instrument, but infinitely second-hand,
And if I have not got phthisis it is only an accident.
Droll phenomena!

POINTS AND LINES

Instants in the quiet, small sharp stars,
Pierce my spirit with a thrust whose speed
Baffles even the grasp of time.
Oh that I might reflect them
As swiftly, as keenly as they shine.
But I am a pool of waters, summer-still,
And the stars are mirrored across me;
Those stabbing points of the sky
Turned to a thread of shaken silver,
A long fine thread.

PANIC

The eyes of the portraits on the wall
Look at me, follow me,
Stare incessantly;
I take it their glance means nothing at all?
– Clearly, oh clearly! Nothing at all . . .

Out in the gardens by the lake
The sleeping peacocks suddenly wake;
Out in the gardens, moonlit and forlorn,
Each of them sounds his mournful horn:
Shrill peals that waver and crack and break.
What can have made the peacocks wake?

RETURN FROM BUSINESS

Evenings in trains,
When the little black twittering ghosts
Along the brims of cuttings,
Against the luminous sky,
Interrupt with their hurrying rumour every thought
Save that one is young and setting,
Headlong westering,
And there is no recapture.

STANZAS

Thought is an unseen net wherein our mind
Is taken and vainly struggles to be free:
Words, that should loose our spirit, do but bind
New fetters on our hoped-for liberty:
And action bears us onward like a stream
Past fabulous shores, scarce seen in our swift course;
Glorious – and yet its headlong currents seem
But backwaters of some diviner force.

There are slow curves, more subtle far than thought,
That stoop to carry the grace of a girl's breast;
And hanging flowers, so exquisitely wrought
In airy metal, that they seem possessed
Of souls; and there are distant hills that lift

72

The shoulder of a god towards the light;
And arrowy trees, sudden and sharp and swift,
Piercing the spirit deeply with delight.

Would I might make these miracles my own!
Like a pure angel, thinking colour and form,
Hardening to rage in a flame of chiselled stone,
Spilling my love like sunlight, golden and warm
On noonday flowers, speaking thè song of birds
Among the branches, whispering the fall of rain,
Beyond all thought, past action and past words,
I would live in beauty, free from self and pain.

POEM

Books and a coloured skein of thoughts were mine;
And magic words lay ripening in my soul
Till their much-whispered music turned a wine
Whose subtlest power was all in my control.

These things were mine, and they were real for me
As lips and darling eyes and a warm breast:
For I could love a phrase, a melody,
Like a fair woman, worshipped and possessed.

I scorned all fire that outward of the eyes
Could kindle passion; scorned, yet was afraid;
Feared, and yet envied those more deeply wise
Who saw the bright earth beckon and obeyed.

But a time came when, turning full of hate
And weariness from my remembered themes,
I wished my poet's pipe could modulate
Beauty more palpable than words and dreams.

73

All loveliness with which an act informs
The dim uncertain chaos of desire
Is mine to-day; it touches me, it warms
Body and spirit with its outward fire.

I am mine no more: I have become a part
Of that great earth that draws a breath and stirs
To meet the spring. But I could wish my heart
Were still a winter of frosty gossamers.

SCENES OF THE MIND

I have run where festival was loud
With drum and brass among the crowd
Of panic revellers, whose cries
Affront the quiet of the skies;
Whose dancing lights contract the deep
Infinity of night and sleep
To a narrow turmoil of troubled fire.
And I have found my heart's desire
In beechen caverns that autumn fills
With the blue shadowiness of distant hills;
Whose luminous grey pillars bear
The stooping sky: calm is the air,
Nor any sound is heard to mar
That crystal silence – as from far,
Far off a man may see
The busy world all utterly
Hushed as an old memorial scene.
Long evenings I have sat and been
Strangely content, while in my hands
I held a wealth of coloured strands,
Shimmering plaits of silk and skeins
Of soft bright wool. Each colour drains
New life at the lamp's round pool of gold;
Each sinks again when I withhold

The quickening radiance, to a wan
And shadowy oblivion
Of what it was. And in my mind
Beauty or sudden love has shined
And wakened colour in what was dead
And turned to gold the sullen lead
Of mean desires and everyday's
Poor thoughts and customary ways.
Sometimes in lands where mountains throw
Their silent spell on all below,
Drawing a magic circle wide
About their feet on every side,
Robbed of all speech and thought and act,
I have seen God in the cataract.
In falling water and in flame,
Never at rest, yet still the same,
God shows himself. And I have known
The swift fire frozen into stone,
And water frozen changelessly
Into the death of gems. And I
Long sitting by the thunderous mill
Have seen the headlong wheel made still,
And in the silence that ensued
Have known the endless solitude
Of being dead and utterly nought.
Inhabitant of mine own thought,
I look abroad, and all I see
Is my creation, made for me:
Along my thread of life are pearled
The moments that make up the world.

L'APRÈS-MIDI D'UN FAUNE

(From the French of Stéphane Mallarmé)

I would immortalize these nymphs: so bright
Their sunlit colouring, so airy light,
It floats like drowsing down. Loved I a dream?
My doubts, born of oblivious darkness, seem
A subtle tracery of branches grown
The tree's true self – proving that I have known
No triumph, but the shadow of a rose.
But think. These nymphs, their loveliness . . . suppose
They bodied forth your senses' fabulous thirst?
Illusion! which the blue eyes of the first,
As cold and chaste as is the weeping spring,
Beget: the other, sighing, passioning,
Is she the wind, warm in your fleece at noon?
No, through this quiet, when a weary swoon
Crushes and chokes the latest faint essay
Of morning, cool against the encroaching day,
There is no murmuring water, save the gush
Of my clear fluted notes; and in the hush
Blows never a wind, save that which through my reed
Puffs out before the rain of notes can speed
Upon the air, with that calm breath of art
That mounts the unwrinkled zenith visibly,
Where inspiration seeks its native sky.
You fringes of a calm Sicilian lake,
The sun's own mirror which I love to take,
Silent beneath your starry flowers, tell
How here I cut the hollow rushes, well
Tamed by my skill, when on the glaucous gold
Of distant lawns about their fountain cold
A living whiteness stirs like a lazy wave;
And at the first slow notes my panpipes gave
These flocking swans, these naiads, rather, fly
Or dive. Noon burns inert and tawny dry,
Nor marks how clean that Hymen slipped away
From me who seek in song the real A.

Wake, then, to the first ardour and the sight,
O lonely faun, of the old fierce white light,
With, lilies, one of you for innocence.
Other than their lips' delicate pretence,
The light caress that quiets treacherous lovers,
My breast, I know not how to tell, discovers
The bitten print of some immortal's kiss.
But hush! a mystery so great as this
I dare not tell, save to my double reed,
Which, sharer of my every joy and need,
Dreams down its cadenced monologues that we
Falsely confuse the beauties that we see
With the bright palpable shapes our song creates:
My flute, as loud as passion modulates,
Purges the common dream of flank and breast,
Seen through closed eyes and inwardly caressed,
Of every empty and monotonous line.

Bloom then, O Syrinx, in thy flight malign,
A reed once more beside our trysting-lake.
Proud of my music, let me often make
A song of goddesses and see their rape
Profanely done on many a painted shape.
So when the grape's transparent juice I drain,
I quell regret for pleasures past and feign
A new real grape. For holding towards the sky
The empty skin, I blow it tight and lie
Dream-drunk till evening, eyeing it.
                              Tell o'er
Remembered joys and plump the grape once more.
Between the reeds I saw their bodies gleam
Who cool no mortal fever in the stream
Crying to the woods the rage of their desire:
And their bright hair went down in jewelled fire
Where crystal broke and dazzled shudderingly.
I check my swift pursuit: for see where lie,
Bruised, being twins in love, by languor sweet,
Two sleeping girls, clasped at my very feet.

I seize and run with them, nor part the pair,
Breaking this covert of frail petals, where
Roses drink scent of the sun and our light play
'Mid tumbled flowers shall match the death of day.
I love that virginal fury – ah, the wild
Thrill when a maiden body shrinks, defiled,
Shuddering like arctic light, from lips that sear
Its nakedness . . . the flesh in secret fear!
Contagiously through my linked pair it flies
Where innocence in either, struggling, dies,
Wet with fond tears or some less piteous dew.
Gay in the conquest of these fears, I grew
So rash that I must needs the sheaf divide
Of ruffled kisses heaven itself had tied.
For as I leaned to stifle in the hair
Of one my passionate laughter (taking care
With a stretched finger, that her innocence
Might stain with her companion's kindling sense
To touch the younger little one, who lay
Child-like unblushing) my ungrateful prey
Slips from me, freed by passion's sudden death,
Nor heeds the frenzy of my sobbing breath.

Let it pass! others of their hair shall twist
A rope to drag me to those joys I missed.
See how the ripe pomegranates bursting red
To quench the thirst of the mumbling bees have bled;
So too our blood, kindled by some chance fire,
Flows for the swarming legions of desire.
At evening, when the woodland green turns gold
And ashen grey, 'mid the quenched leaves, behold!
Red Etna glows, by Venus visited,
Walking the lava with her snowy tread
Whene'er the flames in thunderous slumber die.
I hold the goddess!

                              Ah, sure penalty!

But the unthinking soul and body swoon
At last beneath the heavy hush of noon.
Forgetful let me lie where summer's drouth
Sifts fine the sand and then with gaping mouth
Dream planet-struck by the grape's round wine-red star.

Nymphs, I shall see the shade that now you are.

THE LOUSE-HUNTERS

(From the French of Rimbaud)

When the child's forehead, full of torments red,
Cries out for sleep and its pale host of dreams,
His two big sisters come unto his bed,
Having long fingers, tipped with silvery gleams.

They set him at a casement, open wide
On seas of flowers that stir in the blue airs,
And through his curls, all wet with dew, they slide
Those terrible searching finger-tips of theirs.

He hears them breathing, softly, fearfully,
Honey-sweet ruminations, slow respired:
Then a sharp hiss breaks time and melody –
Spittle indrawn, old kisses new-desired.

Down through the perfumed silences he hears
Their eyelids fluttering: long fingers thrill,
Probing a lassitude bedimmed with tears,
While the nails crunch at every louse they kill.

He is drunk with Languor – soft accordion-sigh,
Delirious wine of Love in Idleness;
Longings for tears come welling up and die,
As slow or swift he feels their magical caress.

3
Leda
(1920)

LEDA

Brown and bright as an agate, mountain-cool,
Eurotas singing slips from pool to pool;
Down rocky gullies; through the cavernous pines
And chestnut groves; down where the terraced vines
And gardens overhang; through valleys grey
With olive trees, into a soundless bay
Of the Aegean. Silent and asleep
Lie those pools now: but where they dream most deep,
Men sometimes see ripples of shining hair
And the young grace of bodies pale and bare,
Shimmering far down – the ghosts these mirrors hold
Of all the beauty they beheld of old,
White limbs and heavenly eyes and the hair's river of gold,
For once these banks were peopled: Spartan girls
Loosed here their maiden girdles and their curls,
And stooping o'er the level water stole
His darling mirror from the sun through whole
Rapturous hours of gazing.
                                        The first star
Of all this milky constellation, far
Lovelier than any nymph of wood or green,
Was she whom Tyndarus had made his queen
For her sheer beauty and subtly moving grace –
Leda, the fairest of our mortal race.
Hymen had lit his torches but one week
About her bed (and still o'er her young cheek
Passed rosy shadows of those thoughts that sped
Across her mind, still virgin, still unwed,
For all her body was her own no more),
When Leda with her maidens to the shore
Of bright Eurotas came, to escape the heat
Of summer noon in waters coolly sweet.
By a brown pool which opened smooth and clear

Below the wrinkled water of a weir
They sat them down under an old fir-tree
To rest: and to the laughing melody
Of their sweet speech the river's rippling bore
A liquid burden, while the sun did pour
Pure colour out of heaven upon the earth.
The meadows seethed with the incessant mirth
Of grasshoppers, seen only when they flew
Their curves of scarlet or sudden dazzling blue.
Within the fir-tree's round of unpierced shade
The maidens sat with laughter and talk, or played,
Gravely intent, their game of knuckle-bones;
Or tossed from hand to hand the old dry cones
Littered about the tree. And one did sing
A ballad of some far-off Spartan king,
Who took a wife, but left her, well-away!
Slain by his foes upon their wedding-day.
"That was a piteous story," Leda sighed,
"To be a widow ere she was a bride."
"Better," said one, "to live a virgin life
Alone, and never know the name of wife
And bear the ugly burden of a child
And have great pain by it. Let me live wild,
A bird untamed by man!" "Nay," cried another,
"I would be wife, if I should not be mother.
Cypris I honour; let the vulgar pay
Their gross vows to Lucina when they pray.
Our finer spirits would be blunted quite
By bestial teeming; but Love's rare delight
Wings the rapt soul towards Olympus' height."
"Delight?" cried Leda. "Love to me has brought
Nothing but pain and a world of shameful thought.
When they say love is sweet, the poets lie;
'Tis but a trick to catch poor maidens by.
What are their boasted pleasures? I am queen
To the most royal king the world has seen;
Therefore I should, if any woman might,
Know at its full that exquisite delight.

Yet these few days since I was made a wife
Have held more bitterness than all my life,
While I was yet a child." The great bright tears
Slipped through her lashes. "Oh, my childish years!
Years that were all my own, too sadly few,
When I was happy – and yet never knew
How happy till to-day!" Her maidens came
About her as she wept, whispering her name,
Leda, sweet Leda, with a hundred dear
Caressing words to soothe her heavy cheer.
At last she started up with a fierce pride
Upon her face. "I am a queen," she cried,
"But had forgotten it a while; and you,
Wenches of mine, you were forgetful too.
Undress me. We would bathe ourself." So proud
A queen she stood, that all her maidens bowed
In trembling fear and scarcely dared approach
To do her bidding. But at last the brooch
Pinned at her shoulder is undone, the wide
Girdle of silk beneath her breasts untied;
The tunic falls about her feet, and she
Steps from the crocus folds of drapery,
Dazzlingly naked, into the warm sun.
God-like she stood; then broke into a run,
Leaping and laughing in the light, as though
Life through her veins coursed with so swift a flow
Of generous blood and fire that to remain
Too long in statued queenliness were pain
To that quick soul, avid of speed and joy.
She ran, easily bounding, like a boy,
Narrow of haunch and slim and firm of breast.
Lovelier she seemed in motion than at rest,
If that might be, when she was never less,
Moving or still, than perfect loveliness.
At last, with cheeks afire and heaving flank,
She checked her race, and on the river's bank
Stood looking down at her own echoed shape
And at the fish that, aimlessly agape,

Hung midway up their heaven of flawless glass,
Like angels waiting for eternity to pass.
Leda drew breath and plunged; her gasping cry
Splashed up; the water circled brokenly
Out from that pearly shudder of dipped limbs;
The glittering pool laughed up its flowery brims,
And everything, save the poor fish, rejoiced:
Their idiot contemplation of the Moist,
The Cold, the Watery, was in a trice
Ended when Leda broke their crystal paradise.

Jove in his high Olympian chamber lay
Hugely supine, striving to charm away
In sleep the long, intolerable noon.
But heedless Morpheus still withheld his boon,
And Jove upon his silk-pavilioned bed
Tossed wrathful and awake. His fevered head
Swarmed with a thousand fancies, which forecast
Delights to be, or savoured pleasures past.
Closing his eyes, he saw his eagle swift,
Headlong as his own thunder, stoop and lift
On pinions upward labouring the prize
Of beauty ravished for the envious skies.
He saw again that bright, adulterous pair,
Trapped by the limping husband unaware,
Fast in each other's arms, and faster in the snare –
And laughed remembering. Sometimes his thought
Went wandering over the earth and sought
Familiar places – temples by the sea,
Cities and islands; here a sacred tree
And there a cavern of shy nymphs.
                                    He rolled
About his bed, in many a rich fold
Crumpling his Babylonian coverlet,
And yawned and stretched. The smell of his own sweat
Brought back to his mind his Libyan desert-fane
Of mottled granite, with its endless train
Of pilgrim camels, reeking towards the sky

Ammonian incense to his hornèd deity;
The while their masters worshipped, offering
Huge teeth of ivory, while some would bring
Their Ethiop wives – sleek wineskins of black silk,
Jellied and huge from drinking asses' milk
Through years of tropical idleness, to pray
For offspring (whom he ever sent away
With prayers unanswered, lest their ebon race
Might breed and blacken the earth's comely face).
Noon pressed on him a hotter, heavier weight.
O Love in Idleness! how celibate
He felt! Libido like a nemesis
Scourged him with itching memories of bliss.
The satin of imagined skin was sleek
And supply warm against his lips and cheek,
And deep within soft hair's dishevelled dusk
His eyelids fluttered; like a flowery musk
The scent of a young body seemed to float
Faintly about him, close and yet remote –
For perfume and the essence of music dwell
In other worlds among the asphodel
Of unembodied life. Then all had flown;
His dream had melted. In his bed, alone,
Jove sweating lay and moaned, and longed in vain
To still the pulses of his burning pain.
In sheer despair at last he leapt from bed,
Opened the window and thrust forth his head
Into Olympian ether. One fierce frown
Rifted the clouds, and he was looking down
Into a gulf of azure calm; the rack
Seethed round about, tempestuously black;
But the god's eye could hold its angry thunders back.
There lay the world, down through the chasmèd blue,
Stretched out from edge to edge unto his view:
And in the midst, bright as a summer's day
At breathless noon, the Mediterranean lay;
And Ocean round the world's dim fringes tossed
His glaucous waves in mist and distance lost;

And Pontus and the livid Caspian Sea
Stirred in their nightmare sleep uneasily.
And 'twixt the seas rolled the wide fertile land,
Dappled with green and tracts of tawny sand,
And rich, dark fallows and fields of flowers aglow,
And the white, changeless silences of snow;
While here and there towns, like a living eye
Unclosed on earth's blind face, towards the sky
Glanced their bright conscious beauty. Yet the sight
Of his fair earth gave him but small delight
Now in his restlessness: its beauty could
Do nought to quench the fever in his blood.
Desire lends sharpness to his searching eyes;
Over the world his focused passion flies
Quicker than chasing sunlight on a day
Of storm and golden April. Far away
He sees the tranquil rivers of the East,
Mirrors of many a strange barbaric feast,
Where un-Hellenic dancing-girls contort
Their yellow limbs, and gibbering masks make sport
Under the moons of many-coloured light
That swing their lantern-fruitage in the night
Of overarching trees. To him it seems
An alien world, peopled by insane dreams.
But these are nothing to the monstrous shapes –
Not men so much as bastardy of apes –
That meet his eyes in Africa. Between
Leaves of grey fungoid pulp and poisonous green,
White eyes from black and browless faces stare.
Dryads with star-flowers in their wooly hair
Dance to the flaccid clapping of their own
Black dangling dugs through forests overgrown,
Platted with writhing creepers. Horrified,
He sees them how they leap and dance, or glide,
Glimpse after black glimpse of a satin skin,
Among unthinkable flowers, to pause and grin
Out through a trellis of suppurating lips,
Of mottled tentacles barbed at the tips

And bloated hands and wattles and red lobes
Of pendulous gristle and enormous probes
Of pink and slashed and tasselled flesh . . .
                              He turns
Northward his sickened sight. The desert burns
All life away. Here in the forkéd shade
Of twin-humped towering dromedaries laid,
A few gaunt folk are sleeping: fierce they seem
Even in sleep, and restless as they dream.
He would be fearful of a desert bride
As of a brown asp at his sleeping side,
Fearful of her white teeth and cunning arts.
Further, yet further, to the ultimate parts
Of the wide earth he looks, where Britons go
Painted among their swamps, and through the snow
Huge hairy snuffling beasts pursue their prey –
Fierce men, as hairy and as huge as they.

Bewildered furrows deepen the Thunderer's scowl;
This world so vast, so variously foul –
Who can have made its ugliness? In what
Revolting fancy were the Forms begot
Of all these monsters? What strange deity –
So barbarously not a Greek! – was he
Who could mismake such beings in his own
Distorted image. Nay, the Greeks alone
Were men; in Greece alone were bodies fair,
Minds comely. In that all-but-island there,
Cleaving the blue sea with its promontories,
Lies the world's hope, the seed of all the glories
That are to be; there, too, must surely live
She who alone can medicinably give
Ease with her beauty to the Thunderer's pain.
Downwards he bends his fiery eyes again,
Glaring on Hellas. Like a beam of light,
His intent glances touch the mountain height
With passing flame and probe the valleys deep,
Rift the dense forest and the age-old sleep

Of vaulted antres on whose pebbly floor
Gallop the loud-hoofed Centaurs; and the roar
Of more than human shouting underground
Pulses in living palpable waves of sound
From wall to wall, until it rumbles out
Into the air; and at that hollow shout
That seems an utterance of the whole vast hill,
The shepherds cease their laughter and are still.
Cities asleep under the noonday sky
Stir at the passage of his burning eye;
And in their huts the startled peasants blink
At the swift flash that bursts through every chink
Of wattled walls, hearkening in fearful wonder
Through lengthened seconds for the crash of thunder –
Which follows not: they are the more afraid.
Jove seeks amain. Many a country maid,
Whose sandalled feet pass down familiar ways
Among the olives, but whose spirit strays
Through lovelier lands of fancy, suddenly
Starts broad awake out of her dream to see
A light that is not of the sun, a light
Darted by living eyes, consciously bright;
She sees and feels it like a subtle flame
Mantling her limbs with fear and maiden shame
And strange desire. Longing and terrified,
She hides her face, like a new-wedded bride
Who feels rough hands that seize and hold her fast;
And swooning falls. The terrible light has passed;
She wakes; the sun still shines, the olive trees
Tremble to whispering silver in the breeze
And all is as it was, save she alone
In whose dazed eyes this deathless light has shone:
For never, never from this day forth will she
In earth's poor passion find felicity,
Or love of mortal man. A god's desire
Has searched her soul; nought but the same strong fire
Can kindle the dead ash to life again,
And all her years will be a lonely pain.

Many a thousand had he looked upon,
Thousands of mortals, young and old, but none –
Virgin, or young ephebus, or the flower
Of womanhood culled in its full-blown hour –
Could please the Thunderer's sight or touch his mind;
The longed-for loveliness was yet to find.
Had beauty fled, and was there nothing fair
Under the moon? The fury of despair
Raged in the breast of heaven's Almighty Lord;
He gnashed his foamy teeth and rolled and roared
In bull-like agony. Then a great calm
Descended on him: cool and healing balm
Touched his immortal fury. He had spied
Young Leda where she stood, poised on the river-side.

Even as she broke the river's smooth expanse,
Leda was conscious of that hungry glance,
And knew it for an eye of fearful power
That did so hot and thunderously lour,
She knew not whence, on her frail nakedness.
Jove's heart held but one thought: he must possess
That perfect form or die – possess or die.
Unheeded prayers and supplications fly,
Thick as a flock of birds, about his ears,
And smoke of incense rises; but he hears
Nought but the soft falls of that melody
Which is the speech of Leda; he can see
Nought but that almost spiritual grace
Which is her body, and that heavenly face
Where gay, sweet thoughts shine through, and eyes are bright
With purity and the soul's inward light.
Have her he must: the teasel-fingered burr
Sticks not so fast in a wild beast's tangled fur
As that insistent longing in the soul
Of mighty Jove. Gods, men, earth, heaven, the whole
Vast universe was blotted from his thought
And nought remained but Leda's laughter, nought
But Leda's eyes. Magnified by his lust,

She was the whole world now; have her he must, he must . . .
His spirit worked; how should he gain his end
With most deliciousness? What better friend,
What counsellor more subtle could he find
Than lovely Aphrodite, ever kind
To hapless lovers, ever cunning, too,
In all the tortuous ways of love to do
And plan the best? To Paphos then! His will
And act were one; and straight, invisible,
He stood in Paphos, breathing the languid air
By Aphrodite's couch. O heavenly fair
She was, and smooth and marvellously young!
On Tyrian silk she lay, and purple hung
About her bed in folds of fluted light
And shadow, dark as wine. Two doves, more white
Even than the white hand on the purple lying
Like a pale flower wearily dropped, were flying
With wings that made an odoriferous stir,
Dropping faint dews of bakkaris and myrrh,
Musk and the soul of sweet flowers cunningly
Ravished from transient petals as they die.
Two stripling cupids on her either hand
Stood near with winnowing plumes and gently fanned
Her hot, love-fevered cheeks and eyelids burning.
Another, crouched at the bed's foot, was turning
A mass of scattered parchments – vows or plaints
Or glad triumphant thanks which Venus' saints,
Martyrs and heroes, on her altars strewed
With bitterest tears or gifts of gratitude.
From the pile heaped at Aphrodite's feet
The boy would take a leaf, and in his sweet,
Clear voice would read what mortal tongues can tell
In stammering verse of those ineffable
Pleasures and pains of love, heaven and uttermost hell.
Jove hidden stood and heard him read these lines
Of votive thanks –

    Cypris, this little silver lamp to thee
      I dedicate.

It was my fellow-watcher, shared with me
Those swift, short hours, when raised above my fate
In Sphenura's white arms I drank
    Of immortality.
"A pretty lamp, and I will have it placed
Beside the narrow bed of some too chaste
Sister of virgin Artemis, to be
A night-long witness of her cruelty.
Read me another, boy," and Venus bent
Her ear to listen to this short lament.
    Cypris, Cypris, I am betrayed!
    Under the same wide mantle laid
    I found them, faithless, shameless pair!
    Making love with tangled hair.
"Alas," the goddess cried, "nor god, nor man,
Nor medicinable balm, nor magic can
Cast out the demon jealousy, whose breath
Withers the rose of life, save only time and death."
Another sheet he took and read again.
    Farewell to love, and hail the long, slow pain
    Of memory that backward turns to joy.
    O I have danced enough and enough sung;
    My feet shall be still now and my voice mute;
    Thine are these withered wreaths, this Lydian flute,
        Cypris; I once was young.
And piteous Aphrodite wept to think
How fadingly upon death's very brink
Beauty and love take hands for one short kiss –
And then the wreaths are dust, the bright-eyed bliss
Perished, and the flute still. "Read on, read on."
But ere the page could start, a lightning shone
Suddenly through the room, and they were 'ware
Of some great terrible presence looming there.
And it took shape – huge limbs, whose every line
A symbol was of power and strength divine,
And it was Jove.
              "Daughter, I come ," said he,
"For counsel in a case that touches me

Close, to the very life." And he straightway
Told her of all his restlessness that day
And of his sight of Leda, and how great
Was his desire. And so in close debate
Sat two gods, planning their rape; while she,
Who was to be their victim, joyously
Laughed like a child in the sudden breathless chill
And splashed and swam, forgetting every ill
And every fear and all, save only this:
That she was young, and it was perfect bliss
To be alive where suns so goldenly shine,
And bees go drunk with fragrant honey-wine,
And the cicadas sing from morn till night,
And rivers run so cool and pure and bright ...
Stretched all her length, arms under head, she lay
In the deep grass, while the sun kissed away
The drops that sleeked her skin. Slender and fine
As those old images of the gods that shine
With smooth-worn silver, polished through the years
By the touching lips of countless worshippers,
Her body was; and the sun's golden heat
Clothed her in softest flame from head to feet
And was her mantle, that she scarcely knew
The conscious sense of nakedness. The blue,
Far hills and the faint fringes of the sky
Shimmered and pulsed in the heat uneasily,
And hidden in the grass, cicadas shrill
Dizzied the air with ceaseless noise, until
A listener might wonder if they cried
In his own head or in the world outside.
Sometimes she shut her eyelids, and wrapped round
In a red darkness, with the muffled sound
And throb of blood beating within her brain,
Savoured intensely to the verge of pain
Her own young life, hoarded it up behind
Her shuttered lids, until, too long confined,
It burst them open and her prisoned soul
Flew forth and took possession of the whole

94

Exquisite world about her and was made
A part of it. Meanwhile her maidens played,
Singing an ancient song of death and birth,
Seed-time and harvest, old as the grey earth,
And moving to their music in a dance
As immemorial. A numbing trance
Came gradually over her, as though
Flake after downy-feathered flake of snow
Had muffled all her senses, drifting deep
And warm and quiet.
                                    From this all-but sleep
She started into life again; the sky
Was full of a strange tumult suddenly –
Beating of mighty wings and shrill-voiced fear
And the hoarse scream of rapine following near.
In the high windlessness above her flew,
Dazzlingly white on the untroubled blue,
A splendid swan, with outstretched neck and wing
Spread fathom wide, and closely following
An eagle, tawny and black. This god-like pair
Circled and swooped through the calm of upper air,
The eagle striking and the white swan still
'Scaping as though by happy miracle
The imminent talons. For the twentieth time
The furious hunter stooped, to miss and climb
A mounting spiral into the height again.
He hung there poised, eyeing the grassy plain
Far, far beneath, where the girls' upturned faces
Were like white flowers that bloom in open places
Among the scarcely budded woods. And they
Breathlessly watched and waited; long he lay,
Becalmed upon that tideless sea of light,
While the great swan with slow and creaking flight
Went slanting down towards safety, where the stream
Shines through the trees below, with glance and gleam
Of blue aerial eyes that seem to give
Sense to the sightless earth and make it live.
The ponderous wings beat on and no pursuit:

Stiff as the painted kite that guards the fruit,
Afloat o'er orchards ripe, the eagle yet
Hung as at anchor, seeming to forget
His uncaught prey, his rage unsatisfied.
Still, quiet, dead . . . and then the quickest-eyed
Had lost him. Like a star unsphered, a stone
Dropped from the vault of heaven, a javelin thrown,
He swooped upon his prey. Down, down he came,
And through his plumes with a noise of wind-blown flame
Loud roared the air. From Leda's lips a cry
Broke, and she hid her face – she could not see him die,
Her lovely, hapless swan.

                   Ah, had she heard,
Even as the eagle hurtled past, the word
That treacherous pair exchanged. "Peace," cried the swan;
"Peace, daughter. All my strength will soon be gone,
Wasted in tedious flying, ere I come
Where my desire hath set its only home."
"Go," said the eagle, "I have played my part,
Roused pity for your plight in Leda's heart
(Pity the mother of voluptuousness).
Go, father Jove; be happy; for success
Attends this moment."

                 On the queen's numbed sense
Fell a glad shout that ended sick suspense,
Bidding her lift once more towards the light
Her eyes, by pity closed against a sight
Of blood and death – her eyes, how happy now
To see the swan still safe, while far below,
Brought by the force of his eluded stroke
So near to earth that with his wings he woke
A gust whose sudden silvery motion stirred
The meadow grass, struggled the sombre bird
Of rage and rapine. Loud his scream and hoarse
With baffled fury as he urged his course
Upwards again on threshing pinions wide.
But the fair swan, not daring to abide
This last assault, dropped with the speed of fear

Towards the river. Like a winged spear,
Outstretching his long neck, rigid and straight,
Aimed at where Leda on the bank did wait
With open arms and kind, uplifted eyes
And voice of tender pity, down he flies.
Nearer, nearer, terribly swift, he sped
Directly at the queen; then widely spread
Resisting wings, and breaking his descent
'Gainst his own wind, all speed and fury spent,
The great swan fluttered slowly down to rest
And sweet security on Leda's breast.
Menacingly the eagle wheeled above her;
But Leda, like a noble-hearted lover
Keeping his child-beloved from tyrannous harm,
Stood o'er the swan and, with one slender arm
Imperiously lifted, waved away
The savage foe, still hungry for his prey.
Baffled at last, he mounted out of sight
And the sky was void – save for a single white
Swan's feather moulted from a harassed wing
That down, down, with a rhythmic balancing
From side to side dropped sleeping on the air.
Down, slowly down over that dazzling pair,
Whose different grace in union was a birth
Of unimagined beauty on the earth:
So lovely that the maidens standing round
Dared scarcely look. Couched on the flowery ground
Young Leda lay, and to her side did press
The swan's proud-arching opulent loveliness,
Stroking the snow-soft plumage of his breast
With fingers slowly drawn, themselves caressed
By the warm softness where they lingered, loth
To break away. Sometimes against their growth
Ruffling the feathers inlaid like little scales
On his sleek neck, the pointed finger-nails
Rasped on the warm, dry, puckered skin beneath;
And feeling it she shuddered, and her teeth
Grated on edge; for there was something strange

And snake-like in the touch. He, in exchange,
Gave back to her, stretching his eager neck,
For every kiss a little amorous peck;
Rubbing his silver head on her golden tresses,
And with the nip of horny dry caresses
Leaving upon her young white breast and cheek
And arms the red print of his playful beak.
Closer he nestled, mingling with the slim
Austerity of virginal flank and limb
His curved and florid beauty, till she felt
That downy warmth strike through her flesh and melt
The bones and marrow of her strength away.
One lifted arm bent o'er her brow, she lay
With limbs relaxed, scarce breathing, deathly still;
Save when a quick, involuntary thrill
Shook her sometimes with passing shudderings,
As though some hand had plucked the aching strings
Of life itself, tense with expectancy.
And over her the swan shook slowly free
The folded glory of his wings, and made
A white-walled tent of soft and luminous shade
To be her veil and keep her from the shame
Of naked light and the sun's noonday flame.

Hushed lay the earth and the wide, careless sky.
Then one sharp sound, that might have been a cry
Of utmost pleasure or of utmost pain,
Broke sobbing forth, and all was still again.

THE BIRTH OF GOD

Night is a void about me; I lie alone;
And water drips, like an idiot clicking his tongue,
Senselessly, ceaselessly, endlessly drips
Into the waiting silence, grown
Emptier for this small inhuman sound.

My love is gone, my love who is tender and young.
O smooth warm body! O passionate lips!
I have stretched forth hands in the dark and nothing found:
The silence is huge as the sky – I lie alone –
My narrow room, a darkness that knows no bound.

How shall I fill this measureless
Deep void that the taking away
Of a child's slim beauty has made?
Slender she is and small, but the loneliness
She has left is a night no stars allay,
And I am cold and afraid.

Long, long ago, cut off from the wolfish pack,
From the warm, immediate touch of friends and mate,
Lost and alone, alone in the utter black
Of a forest night, some far-off, beast-like man,
Cowed by the cold indifferent hate
Of the northern silence, crouched in fear,
When through his bleared and suffering mind
A sudden tremor of comfort ran,
And the void was filled by a rushing wind,
And he breathed a sense of something friendly and near,
And in privation the life of God began.

Love, from your loss shall a god be born to fill
The emptiness, where once you were,
With friendly knowledge and more than a lover's will
To ease despair?
Shall I feed longing with what it hungers after,
Seeing in earth and sea and air
A lover's smiles, hearing a lover's laughter,
Feeling love everywhere?

The night drags on. Darkness and silence grow,
And with them my desire has grown,
My bitter need. Alas, I know,
I know that here I lie alone.

ON HAMPSTEAD HEATH

Beneath the sunlight and blue of all-but Autumn
  The grass sleeps goldenly; woodland and distant hill
Shine through the gauzy air in a dust of golden pollen.
  And even the glittering leaves are almost still.

Scattered on the grass, like a ragman's bundles carelessly dropped,
  Men sleep outstretched or, sprawling, bask in the sun;
Here glows a woman's bright dress and here a child is sitting,
  And I lie down and am one of the sleepers, one

Like the rest of this tumbled crowd. Do they all, I wonder,
  Feel anguish grow with the calm day's slow decline,
Longing, as I, for a shattering wind, a passion
  Of bodily pain to be the soul's anodyne?

SYMPATHY

  The irony of being two ... !
  Grey eyes, wide open suddenly,
  Regard me and enquire; I see a face
  Grave and unquiet in tenderness.
  Heart-rending question of women – never answered:
  "Tell me, tell me, what are you thinking of?"
  Oh, the pain and foolishness of love!
  What can I do but make my old grimace,
  Ending it with a kiss, as I always do?

MALE AND FEMALE CREATED HE THEM

  Diaphenia, drunk with sleep,
  Drunk with pleasure, drunk with fatigue,
  Feels her Corydon's fingers creep –

Ring-finger, middle finger, index, thumb –
Strummingly over the smooth sleek drum
Of her thorax.

                Meanwhile Händel's Gigue
Turns in Corydon's absent mind
To Yakka-Hoola.

                  She can find
No difference in the thrilling touch
Of one who, now, in everything
Is God-like. "Was there ever such
Passion as ours?"

                His pianoing
Gives place to simple arithmetic's
Simplest constatations: – six
Letters in Gneiss and three in Gnu:
Luncheon to-day cost three and two;
In a year – he couldn't calculate
Three-sixty-five times thirty-eight,
Figuring with printless fingers on
Her living parchment.

                 "Corydon!
I faint, faint, faint at your dear touch.
Say, is it possible . . . to love too much?"

FROM THE PILLAR

Simeon, the withered stylite,
   Sat gloomily looking down
Upon each roof and skylight
   In all the seething town.

And in every upper chamber,
   On roofs, where the orange flowers
Make weary men remember
   The perfume of long-dead hours,

He saw the wine-drenched riot
    Of harlots and human beasts,
And how celestial quiet
    Was shattered by their feasts.

The steam of fetid vices
    From a thousand lupanars,
Like smoke of sacrifices,
    Reeked up to the heedless stars.

And the saint from his high fastness
    Of purity apart
Cursed them and their unchasteness,
    And envied them in his heart.

JONAH

A cream of phosphorescent light
Floats on the wash that to and fro
Slides round his feet – enough to show
Many a pendulous stalactite
Of naked mucus, whorls and wreaths
And huge festoons of mottled tripes
And smaller palpitating pipes
Through which a yeasty liquor seethes.

Seated upon the convex mound
Of one vast kidney, Jonah prays
And sings his canticles and hymns
Making the hollow vault resound
God's goodness and mysterious ways,
Till the great fish spouts music as he swims.

VARIATIONS ON A THEME

Swan, Swan,
Yesterday you were
The whitest of things in this dark winter.
To-day the snow has made of your plumes
An unwashed pocket handkercher,
An unwashed pocket handkercher ...
"Lancashire, to Lancashire!" –
Tune of the antique trains long ago:
Each summer holiday a milestone
Backwards, backwards: –
Tenby, Barmouth, and year by year
All the different hues of the sea,
Blue, green and blue.
But on this river of muddy jade
There swims a yellow swan,
And along the bank the snow lies dazzlingly white.

A MELODY BY SCARLATTI

How clear under the trees,
How softly the music flows,
Rippling from one still pool to another
Into the lake of silence.

A SUNSET

Over against the triumph and the close –
    Amber and green and rose –
        Of this short day,
The pale ghost of the moon grows living-bright
    Once more, as the last light
        Ebbs slowly away.
Darkening the fringes of these western glories
    The black phantasmagories

Of cloud advance
With noiseless footing – vague and villainous shapes,
  Wrapped in their ragged fustian capes,
    Of some grotesque romance.
But overhead where, like a pool between
  Dark rocks, the sky is green
    And clear and deep,
Floats windlessly a cloud, with curving breast
  Flushed by the fiery west,
    In god-like sleep . . .
And in my mind opens a sudden door
  That lets me see once more
    A little room
With night beyond the window, chill and damp,
  And one green-lighted lamp
    Tempering the gloom,
While here within, close to me, touching me
  (Even the memory
    Of my desire
Shakes me like fear), you sit with scattered hair;
  And all your body bare
    Before the fire
Is lapped about with rosy flame . . . But still,
  Here on the lonely hill,
    I walk alone;
Silvery green is the moon's lamp overhead,
  The cloud sleeps warm and red,
    And you are gone.

LIFE AND ART

You have sweet flowers for your pleasure,
  You laugh with the bountiful earth
In its richness of summer treasure:
  Where now are your flowers and your mirth?
Petals and cadenced laughter,
  Each in a dying fall,

Droop out of life; and after
   Is nothing; they were all.

But we from the death of roses
   That three suns perfume and gild
With a kiss, till the fourth discloses
   A withered wreath, have distilled
The fulness of one rare phial,
   Whose nimble life shall outrun
The circling shadow on the dial,
   Outlast the tyrannous sun.

FIRST PHILOSOPHER'S SONG

A poor degenerate from the ape,
   Whose hands are four, whose tail's a limb,
I contemplate my flaccid shape
   And know I may not rival him,

Save with my mind – a nimbler beast
   Possessing a thousand sinewy tails,
A thousand hands, with which it scales,
   Greedy of luscious truth, the greased

Poles and the coco palms of thought,
   Thrids easily through the mangrove maze
Of metaphysics, walks the taut
   Frail dangerous liana ways

That link across wild gulfs remote
   Analogies between tree and tree;
Outruns the hare, outhops the goat;
   Mind fabulous, mind sublime and free!

But oh, the sound of simian mirth!
   Mind, issued from the monkey's womb,
Is still umbilical to earth,
   Earth its home and earth its tomb.

SECOND PHILOSOPHER'S SONG

If, O my Lesbia, I should commit,
Not fornication, dear, but suicide,
My Thames-blown body (Pliny vouches it)
Would drift face upwards on the oily tide
With the other garbage, till it putrefied.

But you, if all your lovers' frozen hearts
Conspired to send you, desperate, to drown –
Your maiden modesty would float face down,
And men would weep upon your hinder parts.

'Tis the Lord's doing. Marvellous is the plan
By which this best of worlds is wisely planned.
One law He made for woman, one for man:
We bow the head and do not understand.

FIFTH PHILOSOPHER'S SONG

A million million spermatozoa,
    All of them alive:
Out of their cataclysm but one poor Noah
    Dare hope to survive.

And among that billion minus one
    Might have chanced to be
Shakespeare, another Newton, a new Donne –
    But the One was Me.

Shame to have ousted your betters thus,
    Taking ark while the others remained outside!
Better for all of us, froward Homunculus,
    If you'd quietly died!

NINTH PHILOSOPHER'S SONG*

God's in His Heaven: He never issues
   (Wise Man!) to visit this world of ours.
Unchecked the cancer gnaws our tissues,
   Stops to lick chops and then again devours.

Those find, who most delight to roam
   'Mid castles of remotest Spain,
That there's, thank Heaven, no place like home;
   So they set out upon their travels again.

Beauty for some provides escape,
   Who gain a happiness in eyeing
The gorgeous buttocks of the ape
   Or Autumn sunsets exquisitely dying.

And some to better worlds than this
   Mount up on wings as frail and misty
As passion's all-too-transient kiss
   (Though afterwards – oh, *omne animal triste*!)

But I, too rational by half
   To live but where I bodily am,
Can only do my best to laugh,
   Can only sip my misery dram by dram.

While happier mortals take to drink,
   A dolorous dipsomaniac,
Fuddled with grief I sit and think,
   Looking upon the bile when it is black.

Then brim the bowl with atrabilious liquor!
   We'll pledge our Empire vast across the flood:
For Blood, as all men know, than Water's thicker,
   But water's wider, thank the Lord, than Blood.

* This poem appeared originally in *Jonah* under the title "Sententious Song"

with minor grammatical variations and with the following stanza inserted between the present third and fourth stanzas:

> Some swoon before the uplifted Host,
>   Or gazing on their navels find
> Both Father, Son and Holy Ghost
>   In that small Ark of Ecstasy confined.

The pamphlet entitled *Jonah* contained 12 poems (4 in French), and 50 copies of it were printed for Christmas, 1917, by the Holywell Press, Oxford.

MORNING SCENE

Light through the latticed blind
Spans the dim intermediate space
With parallels of luminous dust
To gild a nuptial couch, where Goya's mind
Conceived those agonising hands, that hair
Scattered, and half a sunlit bosom bare,
And, imminently above them, a red face
Fixed in the imbecile earnestness of lust.

VERREY'S

Here, every winter's night at eight,
Epicurus lies in state,
Two candles at his head and two
Candles at his feet. A few
Choice spirits watch beneath the vault
Of his dim chapel, where default
Of music fills the pregnant air
With subtler requiem and prayer
Than ever an organ wrought with notes
Spouted from its tubal throats.
Black Ethiopia's Holy Child,
The Cradled Bottle, breathes its mild
Meek spirit on the ravished nose,
The palate and the tongue of those
Who piously partake with me
Of this funereal agape.

FRASCATI'S

Bubble-breasted swells the dome
Of this my spiritual home,
From whose nave the chandelier,
Schaffhausen frozen, tumbles sheer.
We in the round balcony sit,
Lean o'er and look into the pit
Where feed the human bears beneath,
Champing with their gilded teeth.
What negroid holiday makes free
With such priapic revelry?
What songs? What gongs? What nameless rites?
What gods like wooden stalagmites?
What steam of blood or kidney pie?
What blasts of Bantu melody?
Ragtime ... but when the wearied Band
Swoons to a waltz, I take her hand,
And there we sit in blissful calm,
Quietly sweating palm to palm.

Foreword to "Soles Occidere et Redire Possunt"

John Ridley, the subject of this poem, was killed in February 1918.
"If I should perish," he wrote to me only five weeks before his
death, "if I should perish – and one isn't exactly a 'good life' at the
moment – I wish you'd write something about me. It isn't vanity
(for I know you'll do me, if anything, rather less than justice!),
not vanity, I repeat; but that queer irrational desire one has for
immortality of any kind, however short and precarious – for
frankly, my dear, I doubt whether your verses will be so very much
more perennial than brass. Still, they'll be something. One can't, of
course, believe in any *au-delà* for one's personal self; one would
have first to believe in some kind of a friendly god. And as for being
a spiritualist spook, one of those wretched beings who seem to
spend their eternity in trying to communicate with the earth by a

single telephone, where the number is always engaged, and the line chronically out of order – well, all I can say is, Heaven preserve me from such a future life. No, my only hope is you – and a damned poor guarantee for eternity. Don't make of me a khaki image, I beg. I'd rather you simply said of me, as Erasmus did of his brother, "Strenuus compotor, nec scortator ignavus'. I sincerely hope, of course, that you won't have to write the thing at all – hope not, but have very little doubt you will. Good-bye."

The following poem is a tentative and provisional attempt to comply with his request. Ridley was an adolescent, and suffered from that instability of mind "produced by the mental conflict forced upon man by his sensitiveness to herd suggestion on the one hand and to experience on the other" (I quote from Mr. Trotter's memorable work on Herd Instinct), that characteristic instability which makes adolescence so feebly sceptical, so inefficient, so profoundly unhappy. I have fished up a single day from Ridley's forgotten existence. It has a bedraggled air in the sunlight, this poor wisp of Lethean weed. Fortunately, however, it will soon be allowed to drop back into the water, where we shall all, in due course, join it. "The greater part must be content to be as though they had not been."

ALDOUS HUXLEY

SOLES OCCIDERE ET REDIRE POSSUNT

I

Between the drawing of the blind
And being aware of yet another day
There came to him behind
Close, pregnant eyelids, like a flame of blue,
Intense, untroubled by the wind,
A Mediterranean bay,
Bearing a brazen beak and foamless oars
To where, marmoreally smooth and bright,
The steps soar up in one pure flight

From the sea's edge to the palace doors,
That have shut, have shut their valves of bronze –
And the windows too are lifeless eyes.

The galley grated on the stone;
He stepped out – and was alone:
No white-sailed hopes, no clouds, nor swans
To shatter the ocean's calm, to break the sky's.

Up the slow stairs:
                   Did he know it was a dream?
First one foot up, then the other foot,
Shuddering like a mandrake root
That hears the truffle-dog at work
And draws a breath to scream;
To moan, to scream.
                   The gates swing wide,
And it is coolly dark inside,
And corridors stretch out and out,
Joining the ceilings to their floors,
And parallels ring wedding bells
And through a hundred thousand doors
Perspective has abolished doubt.

But one of the doors was shut,
And behind it the subtlest lutanist
Was shaking a broken necklace of tinkling notes,
And somehow it was feminine music.
Strange exultant fear of desire, when hearts
Beat brokenly. He laid his hand on the latch –
And woke among his familiar books and pictures;

Real as his dream? He wondered. Ten to nine.
Thursday. Wasn't he lunching at his aunt's?
Distressing circumstance.
But then he was taking Jenny out to dine,
Which was some consolation. What a chin!

Civilized ten thousand years, and still
No better way than rasping a pale mask
With imminent suicide, steel or obsidian:
Repulsive task!
And the more odious for being quotidian.
If one should live till eighty-five . . .
 And the dead, do they still shave? The horrible
 dead, are they alive?

But that lute, playing across his dream . . .
Quick drops breaking the sleep of the water-
 wheel,
Song and ebbing whisper of a summer stream,
Music's endless inconsequence that would reveal
To souls that listened for it, the all
Unseizable confidence, the mystic Rose,
Could it but find the magical fall
That droops, droops and dies into the perfect
 close . . .
And why so feminine? But one could feel
The unseen woman sitting there behind
The door, making her ceaseless slow appeal
To all that prowls and growls in the caves
 beneath
The libraries and parlours of the mind.
If only one were rational, if only
At least one had the illusion of being so . . .

Nine o'clock. Still in bed. Warm, but how
 lonely!
He wept to think of all those single beds,
Those desperate night-long solitudes,
Those mental Salons full of nudes.
Shelley was great when he was twenty-four.
Eight thousand nights alone – minus, perhaps,
Six, or no! seven, certainly not more.
 Five little bits of heaven
 (Tum-de-rum, de-rum, de-rum),

Five little bits of Heaven and one that was a lapse,
High-priced disgust: it stopped him suddenly
In the midst of laughter and talk with a tingling down
   the spine
(Like infants' impoliteness, a terrible infant's brightness),
And he would shut his eyes so as not to see
His own hot blushes calling him a swine.
Atrocious memory! For memory should be
Of things secure and dead, being past,
Not living and disquieting. At last
He threw the nightmare of his blankets off.

Cloudy ammonia, camels in your bath:
The earth hath bubbles as the water hath:
He was not of them, too, too solidly
Always himself. What foam of kissing lips,
Pouting, parting with the ghost of the seven sips
One smacks for hiccoughs!
                                        Pitiable to be
Quite so deplorably naked when one strips.

There was his scar, a panel of old rose
Slashed in the elegant buff of his trunk hose;
Adonis punctured by his amorous boar,
Permanent souvenir of the Great War.
One of God's jokes, typically good,
That wound of his. How perfect that he should
Have suffered it for – what?

II

Oh, the dear front page of the *Times*!
Chronicle of essential history:
Marriage, birth, and the sly mysteriousness
Of lovers' greetings, of lovers' meetings,
And dirty death, impartially paid
To courage and the old decayed.
But nobody had been born to-day,

Nobody married that he knew,
Nobody died and nobody even killed;
   He felt a little aggrieved –
   Nobody even killed.
But, to make up: "Tuesday, Colchester train:
Wanted Brown Eyes' address, with a view to meeting
   again."
Dear Brown Eyes, it had been nice of her
To talk so friendly to a lonely traveller!
   Why is it nobody ever talks to me?

And now, here was a letter from Helen.
Better to open it rather than thus
Dwell in a long muse and maze
Over the scrawled address and the postmark,
Staring stupidly.
Love – was there no escape?
Was it always there, always there?
The same huge and dominant shape,
Like Windsor Castle leaning over the plain:
And the letter a vista cut through the musing forest,
At the end the old Round Tower,
Singing its refrain:
Here we are, here we are, here we are again!

The life so short, so vast love's science and art,
So many conditions of felicity.
   "Darling, will you become a part
   Of my poor physiology?
   And, my beloved, may I have
   The latchkey of your history?
   And while this corpse is what it is
   Dear, we must share geographies."
So many conditions of felicity.
And now time was a widening gulf and space,
A fixed between, and fate still kept them apart.
Her voice quite gone; distance had blurred her face.
The life so short, so vast love's science and art.

So many conditions – and yet, once,
Four whole days,
Four short days of perishing time,
They had fulfilled them all.
But that was long ago, ah! long ago,
Like the last horse bus, or the Christmas pantomime,
Or the Bells, oh, the Bells, of Edgar Allan Poe.

III

"Helen, your letter, proving, I suppose,
That you exist somewhere in space, who knows?
Somewhere in time, perhaps, arrives this morning,
Reminding me with a note of Lutheran warning
That faith's the test, not works. Works! – any fool
Can do them if he tries to; but what school
Can teach one to credit the ridiculous,
The palpably non-existent? So with us,
Votaries of the copulative cult,
In this affair of love, *quicumque vult*,
Whoever would be saved, must love without
Adjunct of sense or reason, must not doubt
Although the deity be far removed,
Remote, invisible; who is not loved
Best by voluptuous works, but by the faith
That lives in absence and the body's death.
I have no faith, and even in love remain
Agnostic. Are you here? The fact is plain,
Constated by the heavenly vision of you,
Maybe by the mouth's warm touch; and that I
    love you,
I then most surely know, most painfully.
But now you've robbed the temple, leaving me
A poor invisibility to adore,
Now that, alas, you're vanished, gone . . . no more;
You take my drift. I only ask your leave
To be a little unfaithful – not to you,
My dear, to whom I was and will be true,

But to your absence. Hence no cause to grieve;
For absence may be cheated of a kiss –
Lightly and laughing – with no prejudice
To the so longed-for presence, which some day
Will crown the presence of
                    Le Vostre J.
(As dear unhappy Troilus would say)."

IV

Oh, the maggots, the maggots in his brains!
Words, words and words.
A birth of rhymes and the strangest,
The most unlikely superfoetations –
New deep thoughts begot by a jingle upon a pun,
New worlds glimpsed through the window of a word
That has ceased, somehow, to be opaque.
All the muses buzzing in his head.
Autobiography crystallised under his pen, thus:

> "When I was young enough not to know youth,
> I was a Faun whose loves were Byzantine
> Among stiff trees. Before me naked Truth
> Creaked on her intellectual legs, divine
> In being inhuman, and was never caught
> By all my speed; for she could outrun thought.
>
> Now I am old enough to know I am young,
> I chase more plastic beauties, but inspire
> Life in their clay, purity in their dung
> With the creative breath of my desire.
> And utter truth is now made manifest
> When on a certain sleeping face and breast
>
> The moonlight dreams and silver chords are strung,
> And a god's hand touches the aching lyre."

He read it through: a pretty, clinquant thing,
Like bright spontaneous bird-song in the spring,
Instinct with instinct, full of dewy freshness.

116

Yes, he had genius, if he chose to use it;
If he chose to – but it was too much trouble,
And he preferred reading. He lit his pipe,
Opened his book, plunged in and soon was drowned
In pleasant seas ... to rise again and find
One o'clock struck and his unshaven face
Still like a record in a musical box,
And Auntie Loo miles off in Bloomsbury.

V

i

The Open Sesame of "Master John",
And then the broad silk bosom of Aunt Loo.
"Dear John, this is a pleasure. How are you?"
"Well, thanks. Where's Uncle Will?" "Your
    uncle's gone
To Bath for his lumbago. He gets on
As well as anyone can hope to do
At his age – for you know he's seventy-two;
But still, he does his bit. He sits upon

The local Tribunal at home, and takes
Parties of wounded soldiers out in brakes
To see the country. And three times a week
He still goes up to business in the City;
And then, sometimes, at night he has to speak
In Village Halls for the War Aims Committee."

ii

"Well, have you any news about the war?
What do they say in France?" "I daren't repeat
The things they say." "You see we've got some meat
For you, dear John. Really, I think before
To-day I've had no lamb this year. We score
By getting decent vegetables to eat,
Sent up from home. This is a good receipt:
The touch of garlic makes it. Have some more.

Poor Tom was wounded on the twenty-third;
Did you know that? And just to-day I heard
News from your uncle that his nephew James
Is dead – Matilda's eldest boy." "I knew
One of those boys, but I'm so bad at names.
Mine had red hair." "Oh, now, that must be Hugh."

iii

"Colonel McGillicuddy came to dine
Quietly here, a night or two ago.
He's on the Staff and very much in the know
About all sorts of things. His special line
Is Tanks. He says we've got a new design
Of super-Tank, with big guns, that can go
(I think he said) at thirty miles or so
An hour. That ought to make them whine

For peace. He also said, if I remember,
That the war couldn't last beyond September,
Because the Germans' trucks were wearing out
And couldn't be replaced. I only hope
It's true. You know your uncle has no doubt
That the whole thing was plotted by the Pope . . . "

". . . Good-bye, dear John. We *have* had a nice talk.
You must soon come again. Good-bye, Good-bye . . ."

He tottered forth, full of the melancholy
That comes of surfeit, and began to walk
Slowly towards Oxford Street. The brazen sky
Burned overhead. Beneath his feet the stones
Were a grey incandescence, and his bones
Melted within him, and his bowels yearned.

VI

The crowd, the crowd – oh, he could almost cry
To see those myriad faces hurrying by,

And each a strong tower rooted in the past
On dark unknown foundations, each made fast
With locks nobody knew the secret of,
No key could open: save that perhaps love
Might push the bars half back and just peep in –
And see strange sights, it may be. But for him
They were locked donjons, every window bright
With beckoning mystery; and then, Good Night!
The lamp was out, they were passed, they were gone
For ever . . . ever. And one might have been
The hero or the friend long sought, and one
Was the loveliest face his eyes had ever seen,
(Vanished as soon) and he went lonely on.

Then in a sudden fearful vision he saw
The whole world spread before him – a vast sphere
Of seething atoms moving to one law:
"Be individual. Approach, draw near,
Yes, even touch: but never join, never be
Other than your own selves eternally."
And there are tangents, tangents of thought that aim
Out through the gaps between the patterned stars
At some fantastic dream without a name
That like the moon shining through prison bars,
Visits the mind with madness. So they fly,
Those soaring tangents, till the first jet tires,
Failing, faltering half-way up the sky,
And breaks – poor slender fountain that aspires
Against the whole strength of the heavy earth
Within whose womb, darkly, it took birth.

Oh, how remote he walked along the street,
Jostling with other lumps of human meat!

He was so tired. The café doors invite.
Caverned within them, still lingers the night
In shadowy coolness, soothing the seared sight.
He sat there smoking, soulless and wholly crass,

Sunk to the eyes in the warm sodden morass
Of his own guts, wearily, wearily
Ruminating visions of mortality –
Momento Moris from the pink alcove,
Nightmare oppressiveness of profane love.
Cesspool within, and without him he could see
Nothing but mounds of flesh and harlotry.
Like a half-pricked bubble pendulous in space,
The buttered leatheriness of a Jew's face
Looms through cigar-smoke; red and ghastly white,
Death's-head women fascinate the sight.
It was the nightmare of a corpse. Dead, dead . . .
Oh, to wake up, to live again! he fled
From that foul place and from himself.

VII

Twin domes of the Alhambra,
Veiled tenderness of the sky above the Square:
He sat him down in the gardens, under the trees,
And in the dust, with the point of his umbrella,
Drew pictures of the crosses we have to bear.

The poor may starve, the sick have horrible pains –
But there are pale eyes even in the London planes.

Men may make war and money, mischief and love –
But about us are colours and the sky above.

Yes, here, where the golden domes ring clear,
And the planes patiently, hopefully renew
Their green refrain from year to year
To the dim spring burden of London's husky blue,
Here he could see the folly of it. How?
Confine a boundless possible within
The prison of an ineluctable Now?
Go slave to pain, woo forth original sin
Out of her lair – and all by a foolish Act?
Madness! But now, Wordsworth of Leicester Square,

He'd learnt his lesson, learnt by the mere fact
Of the place existing, so finely unaware
Of syphilis and the restless in and out
Of public lavatories, and evening shout
Of winners and disasters, races and war.
Troubles come thick enough. Why call for more
By suiting action to the divine Word?
His spleen was chronic, true; but he preferred
Its subtle agony to the brute force
That tugged the barbs of deep-anchored remorse.
The sunlight wrapped folds of soft golden silk
About him, and the air was warm as milk
Against his skin. Long sitting still had made
Cramped soreness such a pleasure, he was afraid
To shift his tortured limbs, lest he should mar
Life's evenness. London's noise from afar
Smoothed out its harshness to soothe his thoughts asleep,
Sound that made silence much more calm and deep.
The domes of gold, the leaves, emerald bright,
Were intense, piercing arrows of delight.
He did not think; thought was a shallow thing
To his deep sense of life, of mere being.
He looked at his hand, lying there on his knee,
The blue veins branching, the tendons cunningly
Dancing like jacks in a piano if he shook
A knot-boned finger. Only to look and look,
Till he knew it, each hair and every pore –
It seemed enough: what need of anything more?
Thought, a blind alley; action, which at best
Is cudgelling water that goes back to rest
As soon as you give over your violences.
No, wisdom culls the flowers of the five senses,
Savouring the secret sweetness they afford:
Instead of which he had a Medical Board
Next week, and they would pass him fit. Good Lord!

Well, let all pass.

               But one must outdo fate,

Wear clothes more modish than the fashion, run
Faster than time, not merely stand and wait;
Do in a flash what cannot be undone
Through ten eternities. Predestinate?
So would God be – that is, if there were one:
General epidemic which spoils nobody's fun.
Action, action! Quickly rise and do
The most irreparable things; beget,
In one brief consummation of the will,
Remorse, reaction, wretchedness, regret.
Action! This was no time for standing still.

He crushed his hat down over his eyes
And walked with a stamp to symbolise
Action, action – left, right, left;
Planting his feet with a slabby beat,
Taking strange Procrustean steps,
Lengthened, shortened to avoid
Touching the lines between the stones –
A thing which makes God so annoyed.

Action, action! First of all
He spent three pounds he couldn't afford
In buying a book he didn't want,
For the mere sake of having been
Irrevocably extravagant.
Then feeling very bold, he pressed
The bell of a chance house; it might
Disclose some New Arabian Night
Behind its grimy husk, who knows?
The seconds passed; all was dead.
Arrogantly he rang once more.
His heart thumped on sheer silence; but at last
There was a shuffling; something behind the door
Became approaching panic, and he fled.

VIII

"Misery," he said, "to have no chin,
Nothing but brains and sex and taste
Only omissively to sin,
Weakly kind and cowardly chaste.

But when the war is over,
I will go to the East and plant
Tea and rubber, and make much money.
I will eat the black sweat of niggers
And flagellate them with whips.
I shall be enormously myself,
    Incarnate Chin."

The anguish of thinking ill of oneself
(St. Paul's religion, poignant beyond words)
Turns ere you know it to faint minor thirds
Before the ritualistic pomps of the world –
The glass-grey silver of rivers, silken skies unfurled,
Urim and Thummim of dawn and sun-setting,
And the lawn sleeves of a great episcopal cloud,
Matins of song and vesperal murmuring,
Incense of night-long flowers and earth new-ploughed;
All beauties of sweetness and all that shine or sing.
Conscience is soothed by beauty's subtle fingers
Into voluptuousness, where nothing lingers
Of bitterness, saving a sorrow that is
Rather a languor than a sense of pain.

So, from the tunnel of St. Martin's Lane
Sailing into the open Square, he felt
His self-reproach, his good resolutions melt
Into an ecstasy, gentle as balm,
Before the spire, etched black and white on the calm
Of a pale windless sky, St. Martin's spire,
And the shadows sleeping beneath the portico
And the crowd hurrying, ceaselessly, to and fro.

Alas, the bleached and slender tower that aches
Upon the gauzy sky, where blueness breaks
Into sweet hoarseness, veiled with love and tender
As the dove's voice alone in the woods: too slender,
Too finely pencilled – black and bleaching white
On smoky mist, too clear in the keen light
Of utmost summer: and oh! the lives that pass
In one swift stream of colour, too, too bright,
Too swift – and all the lives unknown,
                                        Alone.
                                    Alas . . .

A truce to summer and beauty and the pain
Of being too consciously alive among
The things that pass and the things that remain,
(Oh, equal sadness!) the pain of being young.

Truce, truce . . . Once again he fled; –
All his life, it seemed, was a flight; –
Fled and found
Sanctuary in a cinema house.
Huge faces loomed and burst,
Like bubbles in a black wind.
He shut his eyes on them and in a little
Slept; slept, while the pictures
Passed and returned, passed once more and returned.
And he, like God in the midst of the wheeling world,
Slept on; and when he woke it was eight o'clock.
Jenny? Revenge is sweet; he will have kept
   Dear Jenny waiting.

IX

Tall straight poplars stand in a meadow;
The wind and sun caress them, dappling
The deep green grass with shine and shadow;
And a little apart one slender sapling
Sways in the wind and almost seems

Conscious of its own supple grace,
And shakes its twin-hued leaves and gleams
With silvery laughter, filling the place
Where it stands with a sudden flash of human
Beauty and grace; till from her tree
Steps forth the dryad, now turned woman,
And sways to meet him. It is she.

Food and drink, food and drink:
Olives as firm and sleek and green
As the breasts of a sea-god's daughter,
Swimming far down where the corpses sink
Through the dense shadowy water.
Silver and black on flank and back,
The glossy sardine mourns its head.
The red anchovy and the beetroot red,
With carrots, build a gorgeous stair –
Bronze, apoplexy and Venetian hair –
And the green pallor of the salad round
Sharpens their clarion sound.
  De lady take hors d'oeuvres? and de gentleman too?
  Per due! Due! Echo answers: Du' . . .

"So, Jenny, you've found another Perfect Man."
"Perfect, perhaps; but not so sweet as you,
Not such a baby." "Me? A baby. Why,
I am older than the rocks on which I sit . . . "
  Oh, how delightful, talking about oneself!

Golden wine, pale as a Tuscan primitive,
And wine's strange taste, half loathsome, half delicious:
Come, my Lesbia, let us love and live.
What though the mind still think that one thing's vicious
More than another? If the thought can give
This wine's rich savour to our laughing kiss,
Let us preserve the Christian prejudice.
Oh, there are shynesses and silences,
Shynesses and silences!
But luckily God also gave us wine.

"Jenny, adorable – " (what draws the line
At the mere word "love"?) "has anyone the right
To look so lovely as you look tonight,
To have such eyes, such a helmet of bright hair?"
But candidly, he wondered, do I care?

He heard her voice and himself spoke,
But like faint light through a cloud of smoke,
There came, unreal and far away,
Mere sounds utterly empty – like the drone
Of prayers, *crambe repetita*, prayers and praise,
Long, long ago, in the old School Chapel days;
Senseless, but so intrusive on one's own
Interior life one couldn't even think . . .

O sweet, rare, perilous, retchy drink!
Another glass . . .

X

How cool is the moonless summer night, how sweet
After the noise and the dizzy choking heat!
The bloodless lamps look down upon their own
Green image in the polished roadway thrown,
And onward and out of sight the great road runs,
Smooth and dark as a river of calm bronze.

Freedom and widening space: his life expands,
Ready, it seems, to burst the iron bands
Of self, to fuse with other lives and be
Not one but the world, no longer "I" but "She".

See, like the dolorous memory
Of happy times in misery,
An aged hansom fills the street
With the superannuated beat
Of hollow hoofs and bells that chime
Out of another quieter time.

"Good-night," the last kiss, "and God bless you, my
    dear."
So, she was gone, she who had been so near,
So breathing-warm – soft mouth and hands and hair –
A moment since. Had she really been there,
Close at his side, and had he kissed her? It seemed
Unlikely as something somebody else had dreamed
And talked about at breakfast, being a bore:
Improbable, unsubstantial, dim, yet more
Real than the rest of life; real as the blaze
Of a sudden-seen picture, as the lightning phrase
With which the poet-gods strangely create
Their brief bright world beyond the reach of fate.
Yet he could wonder now if he had kissed
Her or his own loved thoughts. Did she exist
Now she was history and safely stowed
Down in the past? There (with a conscious smile),
There let her rest eternal. And meanwhile,
Lamp-fringed towards meeting parallels, the road
Stretched out and out, and the old weary horse,
Come from the past, went jogging his homeward course
Uphill through time to some demoded place,
On ghostly hoofs back to the safe Has-Been: –
But fact returns insistent as remorse;
Uphill towards Hampstead, back to the year of grace
Nineteen hundred and seventeen.

XI

Between the drawing of the blind
And being aware of yet another day ...

4

The Cicadas and Other Poems

(1931)

The following poems in *The Cicadas and Other Poems* comprise Huxley's 1929 volume, *Arabia Infelix and Other Poems*: "Arabia Infelix", "Noblest Romans", "Meditation", "September", "Seasons", "Picture by Goya: A Highway Robbery", "Theatre of Varieties", "Caligular [*sic*], or the Triumph of Beauty", "Nero and Sporus, or the Triumph of Art", and "Nero and Sporus II", "Mythological Incident", "Femmes Damnées", "The Pergola", "Sheep", "Black Country", "Carpe Noctem", and "The Cicadas".

THEATRE OF VARIETIES

Circle on circle the hanging gardens descend,
Sloping from upper darkness, each flower face
Open, turned to the light and laughter and life
Of the sun-like stage. And all the space between,
Like the hot fringes of a summer sky,
Is quick with trumpets, beats with the pulse of drums,
Athwart whose sultry thunders rise and fall
Flute fountains and the swallow flight of strings.
Music, the revelation and marvellous lie!
On the bright trestles tumblers, tamer of beasts,
Dancers and clowns affirm their fury of life.

> "The World-Renowned Van Hogen Mogen in
> The Master Mystery of Modern Times".

He talks, he talks; more powerfully than even
Music his quick words hammer on men's minds.
"Observe this hat, ladies and gentlemen;
Empty, observe, empty as the universe
Before the Head for which this Hat is made
Was or could think. Empty, observe, observe."
The rabbit kicks; a bunch of paper flowers
Blooms in the limelight; paper tape unrolls,
Endless, a clue. "Ladies and gentlemen ... "
Sharp, sharp on malleable minds his words
Hammer. The little Indian boy
Enters the basket. Bright, an Ethiop's sword
Transfixes it and bleeding is withdrawn.
Death draws and petrifies the watching faces.
"Ladies and gentlemen": the great Van Hogen Mogen
Smiles and is kind. A puddle of dark blood
Slowly expands. "The irremediable
Has been and is no more."
Empty of all but blood, the basket gapes.

"Arise!" he calls, and blows his horn. "Arise!"
And bird-like from the highest gallery
The little Indian answers.
Shout upon shout, the hanging gardens reverberate.
Happy because the irremediable is healed,
Happy because they have seen the impossible,
Because they are freed from the dull daily law,
They shout, they shout. And great Van Hogen Mogen
Modestly bows, graciously smiles. The band
Confirms the lie with cymbals and bassoons,
The curtain falls. How quickly the walls recede,
How soon the petrified gargoyles re-become
Women and men! who fill the warm thick air
With rumour of their loves and discontents,
Not suffering even great Hogen Mogen –
Only begetter out of empty hats
Of rose and rabbit, raiser from the dead –
To invade the sanctity of private life.

The Six Aerial Sisters Polpetini
Dive dangerously from trapeze to far
Trapeze, like stars, and know not how to fall.
For if they did and if, of his silver balls,
Sclopis, the juggler, dropped but one – but one
Of all the flying atoms which he builds
With his quick throwing into a solid arch –
What panic then would shake the pale flower faces
Blooming so tranquilly in their hanging beds!
What a cold blast of fear! But patrons must not,
And since they must not, cannot be alarmed.
Hence Sclopis, hence (the proof is manifest)
The Six Aerial Ones infallibly
Function, and have done, and for ever will.

Professor Chubb's Automaton performs
Upon the viols and virginals, plays chess,
Ombre and loo, mistigri, tric-trac, pushpin,
Sings Lilliburlero in falsetto, answers

Strong and yet bowed, superbly on her knees,
She snuffed her triumph, on that frailer grace
Poring voluptuously, as though to seize
The signs of thanks upon the other's face.

Gazing, she sought in her pale victim's eye
The speechless canticle that pleasure sings,
The infinite gratitude that, like a sigh,
Mounts slowly from the spirit's deepest springs.

"Now, now you understand (for love like ours
Is proof enough) that 'twere a sin to throw
The sacred holocaust of your first flowers
To those whose breath might parch them as they blow.

"Light falls my kiss, as the ephemeral wing
That scarcely stirs the shining of a lake.
What ruinous pain your lover's kiss would bring!
A plough that leaves a furrow in its wake.

"Over you, like a herd of ponderous kine,
Man's love will pass and his caresses fall
Like trampling hooves. Then turn your face to mine;
Turn, oh my heart, my half of me, my all!

"Turn, turn, that I may see their starry lights,
Your eyes of azure; turn. For one dear glance
I will reveal love's most obscure delights,
And you shall drowse in pleasure's endless trance."

"Not thankless, nor repentant in the least
Is your Hippolyta." She raised her head.
"But one who from some grim nocturnal feast
Returns at dawn feels less disquieted.

"I bear a weight of terrors, and dark hosts
Of phantoms haunt my steps and seem to lead.
I walk, compelled, behind these beckoning ghosts
Down sliding roads and under skies that bleed.

"Is ours so strange an act, so full of shame?
Explain the terrors that disturb my bliss.
When you say, Love, I tremble at the name;
And yet my mouth is thirsty for your kiss.

"Ah, look not so, dear sister, look not so!
You whom I love, even though that love should be
A snare for my undoing, even though
Loving I am lost for all eternity."

Delphine looked up, and fate was in her eye.
From the god's tripod and beneath his spell,
Shaking her tragic locks, she made reply:
"Who in love's presence dares to speak of hell?

"Thinker of useless thoughts, let him be cursed,
Who in his folly, venturing to vex
A question answerless and barren, first
With wrong and right involved the things of sex!

"He who in mystical accord conjoins
Shadow with heat, dusk with the noon's high fire,
Shall never warm the palsy of his loins
At that red sun which mortals call desire.

"Go, seek some lubber groom's deflowering lust;
Take him your heart and leave me here despised!
Go – and bring back, all horror and disgust,
The livid breasts man's love has stigmatized.

"One may not serve two masters here below."
But the child answered: "I am torn apart,
I feel my inmost being rent, as though
A gulf had yawned – the gulf that is my heart.

"Naught may this monster's desperate thirst assuage, –
As fire 'tis hot, as space itself profound –
Naught stay the Fury from her quenchless rage,
Who with her torch explores its bleeding wound.

"Curtain the world away and let us try
If lassitude will bring the boon of rest.
In your deep bosom I would sink and die,
Would find the grave's fresh coolness on your breast."

Hence, lamentable victims, get you hence!
Hell yawns beneath, your road is straight and steep.
Where all the crimes receive their recompense
Wind-whipped and seething in the lowest deep

With a huge roaring as of storms and fires,
Go down, mad phantoms, doomed to seek in vain
The ne'er-won goal of unassuaged desires,
And in your pleasures find eternal pain!

Sunless your caverns are; the fever damps
That filter in through every crannied vent
Break out with marsh-fire into sudden lamps
And steep your bodies with their frightful scent.

The barrenness of pleasures harsh and stale
Makes mad your thirst and parches up your skin;
And like an old flag volleying in the gale,
Your whole flesh shudders in the blasts of sin.

Far from your kind, outlawed and reprobate,
Go, prowl like wolves through desert worlds apart!
Disordered souls, fashion your own dark fate,
And flee the god you carry in your heart.

ARABIA INFELIX

Under a ceiling of cobalt
And mirrored by as void a blue,
Wet only with the wind-blown salt,
The Arabian land implores a dew.

143

Parched, parched are the hills, and dumb
That thundering voice of the ravine;
Round the dead springs the birds are seen
No more, no more at evening come

(Like lovely thoughts to one who dwells
In quiet, like enchanting hopes)
The leopards and the shy gazelles
And the light-footed antelopes.

Death starts at every rattling gust
That in the withered torrent's bed
Whirls up a phantom of grey dust
And, dying, lets the ghost fall dead.

Dust in a dance may seem to live;
But laid, not blown, it brings to birth.
Not wind, but only rain can give
Life, and to a patient earth.

Hot wind from this Arabian land
Chases the clouds, withholds the rain.
No footstep prints the restless sand
Wherein who sows, he sows in vain.

If there were water, if there were
But a shower, a little fountain springing,
How rich would be the perfumed air,
And the green woods with shade and singing

Bright hills, but by the sun accursed,
Peaceful, but with the peace of hell –
Once on these barren slopes there fell
A plague more violent than thirst:

Anguish to kill inveterate pain
And mortal slaking of desire;
Dew, and a long-awaited rain –
A dew of blood, a rain of fire.

Into a vacant sky the moist
Gray pledge of spring and coming leaves
Swam, and the thirsty hills rejoiced,
All golden with their future sheaves.

Flower-phantoms in the parching air
Nodded, and trees ungrown were bowed;
With love like madness, like despair,
The mountain yearned towards the cloud.

And she in silence slowly came,
Oh! to transfigure, to renew,
Came laden with a gift of dew,
But with it dropped the lightning's flame;

A flame that rent the crags apart,
But rending made a road between
For water to the mountain's heart,
That left a scar, but left it green.

Faithless the cloud and fugitive;
An empty heaven nor burns, nor wets;
At peace, the barren land regrets
Those agonies that made it live.

THE MOOR

Champion of souls and holiness, upholder
Of all the virtues, father of the Church,
Honest, honest, honest Iago! how
Crusadingly, with what indignant zeal
(*Ora pro nobis*), caracoling on
Your high horse and emblazoned, gules on white,
Did you ride forth (Oh, pray for us), ride forth
Against the dark-skinned hosts of evil, ride,
Martyr and saint, against those paynim hosts,

Having for shield all Sinai, and for sword,
To smite rebellion and avenge the Lord,
The sharp, the shining certainty of faith!
(*Ora pro nobis*) point us out the Way.

> "Lily bright and stinking mud:
> Fair is fair and foul is ill.
> With her, on her, what you will.
> This fire must be put out with blood,
> Put out with blood."

But for a glint, a hint of questing eyes,
Invisible, darkness through darkness goes
On feet that even in their victim's dreaming
Wake not an echo.
Lost, he is lost; and yet thus wholly in darkness
Melted, the Moor is more Othello than when,
Green-glittering, the sharp Venetian day
Revealed him armed and kingly and commanding
Captain of men.

How still she lies, this naked Desdemona,
All but a child and sleeping and alone,
How still and white!
Whose breasts, whose arms, the very trustfulness
Of her closed eyelids and unhurried breath
More than a philtre maddeningly invite
Lust and those hands, those huge dark hands, and death.

> "For oh, the lily and the mud!
> Fair is still fair and foulness, ill.
> With her, on her, what you will.
> This fire must be put out with blood."

Well, now the fire is out, and the light too;
All, all put out. In Desdemona's place
Lies now a carrion. That fixed grimace
Of lidless eyes and starting tongue

Derides his foolishness. Cover her face;
This thing but now was beautiful and young.
Honest Iago's Christian work is over;
Short, short the parleying at the Golden Gate.
"For I am one who made the Night ashamed
Of his own essence, that his dark was dark;
One who with good St. Jerome's filthy tongue
Tainted desire and taught the Moor to scorn
His love's pale body, and because she had
Lain gladly in his arms, to call her whore
And strangle her for whoredom." So he spoke,
And with majestic motion heaven's high door
Rolled musically apart its burnished vans
To grant him entrance.

                Turning back meanwhile
From outer darkness, Othello and his bride
Perceive the globe of heaven like one small lamp
Burning alone at midnight in the abyss
Of some cathedral cavern; pause, and then
With face once more averted, hand in hand,
Explore the unseen treasures of the dark.

NOBLEST ROMANS

Columns and unageing fountains,
Jets of frost and living foam –
Let them leap from seven mountains,
The seven hills of Rome.

Flanked by arch and echoing arch,
Let the streets in triumph go;
Bid the aqueducts to march
Tireless through the plain below.

Column-high in the blue air,
Let the marble Caesars stand;
Let the gods, who living were
Romans, lift a golden hand.

Many, but each alone, a crowd,
Yet of Romans, throng their shrine;
Worshippers themselves divine,
Gods to gods superbly bowed;

Romans bowed to shapes that they,
Sculptors of the mind, set free;
Supplicant that they may be
Peers of those to whom they pray.

ORION

Tree-tangled still, autumn Orion climbs
Up from among the North Wind's shuddering emblems
Into the torrent void
And dark abstraction of invisible power,
The heart and boreal substance of the night.

Pleione flees before him, and behind,
Still sunken, but prophetically near,
Death in the Scorpion hunts him up the sky
And round the vault of time, round the slow-curving year,
Follows unescapably
And to the end, aye, and beyond the end
Will follow, follow; for of all the gods
Death only cannot die.

The rest are mortal. And how many lie
Already with their creatures' ancient dust!
Dead even in us who live – or hardly live,
Since of our hearts impiety has made,

Not tombs indeed (for they are holy; tombs
Secretly live with everlasting Death's
Dark and mysterious life),
But curious shops and learned lumber rooms
Of bone and stone and every mummied thing,
Where Death himself his sacred sting
Forgets (how studiously forgotten
Amid the irrelevant to and fro of feet!),
Where by the peeping and the chattering,
The loud forgetfulness seemingly slain,
He lies with all the rest – and yet we know,
In secret yet we know,
Death is not dead, not dead but only sleeping,
And soon will rise again.

Not so the rest. Only the Scorpion burns
In our unpeopled heaven of empty names
And insubstantial echoes; only Death
Still claims our prayers, and still to those who pray
Returns his own dark blood and quickening breath,
Returns the ominous mystery of fear.
Where are the gods of dancing and desire?
Anger and joy, laughter and tears and wine,
Those other mysteries of fire and flame,
Those more divine than Death's – ah, where are they?
Only a ghost between the shuddering trees,
Only a name and ghostly numbers climb;
And where a god pursued and fled,
Only a ghostly time, a ghostly place
Attends on other ghostly times and places.
Orion and the rest are dead.

And yet to-night, here in the exulting wind,
Amid the enormous laughters of a soul
At once the world's and mine,
God-like Orion and all his brother stars
Shine as with living eyes,
With eyes that glance a recognition, glance a sign

Across the quickened dark, across the gulphs
That separate no more,
But, like wide seas that yet bring home the freight
Of man's mad yearning for a further shore,
Join with a living touch, unbrokenly,
Life to mysterious life,
The Hunter's alien essence to my own.

Orion lives; yet I who know him living,
Elsewhere and otherwise
Know him for dead, and dead beyond all hope,
For 'tis the infertile and unquickening death
Of measured places and recorded times,
The death of names and numbers that he dies.
Only the phantom of Orion climbs.
Put out the eyes, put out the living eyes
And look elsewhere; yes, look and think and be
Elsewhere and otherwise.
But *here* and *thus* are also in their right,
Are in their right divine to send this wind of laughter
Rushing through the cloudless dark
And through my being; have a right divine
And imprescriptible now to reveal
The starry god, the right to make me feel,
As even now, as even now I feel,
His living presence near me in the night.

A curved and figured glass hangs between light and light,
Between the glow within us and the glow
Of what mysterious sun without?
Vast over earth and sky, or focussed burningly
Upon the tender quick, our spirits throw
Each way their images – each way the forms
O! shall it be of beauty, shall it be
The naked skeletons of doubt?
Or else, symbolically dark, the cloudy forms
Of mystery, or dark (but dark with death)
Shapes of sad knowledge and defiling hate?

"Lighten our darkness, Lord." With what pure faith,
What confident hope our fathers once implored
The Light! But 'tis the shitten Lord of Flies
Who with his loathsome bounties now fulfils
On us their prayers. Our fathers prayed for light.
Through windows at their supplication scoured
Bare of the sacred blazons, but instead
Daubed with the dung-god's filth, all living eyes,
Whether of stars or men, look merely dead;
While on the vaulted crystal of the night
Our guttering souls project,
Not the Wild Huntsman, not the Heavenly Hosts,
But only times and places, only names and ghosts.

And yet, for all the learned Lord of Dung,
The choice is ours, the choice is always ours,
To see or not to see the living powers
That move behind the numbered points and times.
The Fly King rules; but still the choice remains
With us his subjects, we are free, are free
To love our fate or loathe it; to rejoice
Or weep or wearily accept; are free,
For all the scouring of our souls, for all
The miring of their crystal, free to give
Even to an empty sky, to vacant names,
Or not to give, our worship; free to turn
Lifewards, within, without, to what transcends
The squalor of our personal ends and aims,
Or not to turn; yes, free to die or live;
Free to be thus and passionately here,
Or otherwise and otherwhere;
Free, in a word, to learn or not to learn
The art to think and musically do
And feel and be, the never more than now
Difficult art harmoniously to live
All poetry – the midnight of Macbeth
And ripe Odysseus and the undying light
Of Gemma's star and Cleopatra's death

And Falstaff in his cups; the art to live
That discipline of flowers, that solemn dance
Of sliding weights and harnessed powers
Which is a picture; or to live the grave
And stoical recession, row on row,
Of equal columns, live the passionate leaping,
The mutual yearning, meeting, marrying,
And then the flame-still rapture, the fierce trance
Of consummation in the Gothic night.

The choice is always ours. Then, let me choose
The longest art, the hard Promethean way
Cherishingly to tend and feed and fan
That inward fire, whose small precarious flame,
Kindled or quenched, creates
The noble or the ignoble men we are,
The worlds we live in and the very fates,
Our bright or muddy star.

Up from among the emblems of the wind
Into its heart of power,
The Huntsman climbs, and all his living stars
Are bright, and all are mine.

MEDITATION

What now caresses you, a year ago
Bent to the wind that sends a travelling wave
Almost of silver through the silky corn
Westward of Calgary; or two weeks since
Bleated in Gloster market, lowed at Thame,
And slowly bled to give my lips desire;
Or in the teeming darkness, fathoms down,
Hung, one of millions, poised between the ooze
And the wind's foamy skirts; or feathered flew,
Or deathwards ran before the following gun.

And all day long, knee deep in the wet grass,
The piebald cows of Edam chewed and chewed,
That what was cheese might pulse thus feverishly;
And now, prophetically, even now
They ponder in their ruminating jaws
My future body, which in Tuscan fields
Yet grows, yet grunts among the acorns, yet
Is salt and iron, water and touchless air,
Is only numbers variously moved,
Is nothing, yet will love your nothingness.
Vast forms of dust, tawny and tall and vague,
March through the desert, creatures of the wind.
Wind, blowing whither, blowing whence, who knows? –
Wind was the soul that raised them from the sand,
Moved and sustained their movement, and at last
Abating, let them fall in separate grains
Slowly to earth and left an empty sky.

SEPTEMBER

Spring is past and over these many days,
Spring and summer. The leaves of September droop,
Yellowing and all but dead on the patient trees.
Nor is there any hope in me. I walk
Slowly homewards. Night is empty and dark
Behind my eyes as it is dark without
And empty round about me and over me.
Spring is past and over these many days,
But, looking up, suddenly I see
Leaves in the upthrown light of a street lamp shining,
Clear and luminous, young and so transparent,
They seem but the coloured foam of air, green fire,
No more than the scarce-embodied thoughts of leaves.
And it is spring within that circle of light.

Oh, magical brightness! The old leaves are made new.
In the mind, too, some coloured accident
Of beauty revives and makes all young again,
A chance light shines and suddenly it is spring.

SEASONS

Blood of the world, time stanchless flows;
The wound is mortal and is mine.
I act, but not to my design,
Choose, but 'twas ever fate that chose,
Would flee, but there are doors that close.
Winter has set its muddy sign
Without me and within. The rose
Dies also in my heart and no stars shine.

But nightingales call back the sun;
The doors are down and I can run,
Can laugh, for destiny is dead.
All springs are hoarded in the flowers;
Quick flow the intoxicating hours,
For wine as well as blood is red.

STORM AT NIGHT

Oh, how aquarium-still, how brooding-warm
This paradise! How peacefully in the womb
Of war itself, and at the heart of storm
How safely – safely a captive, in a tomb –
I lie and, listening to the wild assault,
The pause and once-more fury of the gale,
Feel through the cracks of my sepulchral vault
The fine-drawn probe of air, and watch the pale
Unearthly lightnings leaps across the sky

Like sudden sperm and die and leap again.
The thunder calls and every spasm of fire
Beckons, a signal, to that old desire
In calm for tempest and at ease for pain.
Dreaming of strength and courage, here I lie.

MEDITERRANEAN

This tideless sapphire uniformly brims
Its jewelled circle of Tyrrhenian shore.
No vapours tarnish, not a cloud bedims,
And time descending only more and more
Makes rich, makes deep the unretiring gem.
And yet for me who look on it, how wide
The world of mud to which my thoughts condemn
This loathing vision of a sunken tide!
The ebb is mine. Life to its lowest neap
Withdrawn reveals that black and hideous shoal
Where I lie stranded. Oh deliver me
From this defiling death! Moon of the soul,
Call back the tide that ran so strong and deep,
Call back the shining jewel of the sea.

TIDE

And if the tide should be for ever low,
The silted channels turned to ooze and mire?
And this grey delta – if it still should grow,
Bank after bank, and still the sea retire?
Retire beyond the halcyon hopes of noon
And silver night, the thread of wind and wave,
Past all the dark compulsion of the moon,
Past resurrection, past her power to save?
There is a firm consenting to disaster,
Proud resignation to accepted pain.

Pain quickens him who makes himself its master,
And quickening battle crowns both loss and gain.
But to this silting of the soul, who gives
Consent is no more man, no longer lives.

FÊTE NATIONALE

These lamps, like some miraculous gift of rain,
Evoke an April from the dusty weight
Of leaves that hang resigned and know their fate,
Expecting autumn: they are young again.
And young these dancers underneath the trees
Who pass and pass, how many all at one!
Like things of wax beneath an Indian sun,
Melted in music. Oh, to be one of these,
Of these the born inhabitants of earth,
Each other's joyful captives! Oh, to be
Safe home from those far islands, where the free,
Whose exile buys the honour of their birth,
Hark back across the liberating sea
To the lost continent of tears and mirth!

MIDSUMMER DAY

This day was midsummer, the longest tarrying
Time makes between two sleeps. What have I done
With this longest of so few days, how spent,
Dear God, the golden, golden gift of sun?
Virginal, when I rose, the morning lay
Ready for beauty's rape, for wisdom's marrying.
I wrote: only an inky spider went,
Smear after smear, across the unsullied day.

If there were other places, if there were
But other days than this longest of few;
If one had courage, did one dare to do
That which alone might kill what now defaces
This the one place of all the countless places,
This only day when one will never dare!

AUTUMN STILLNESS

Gray is the air and silent as the sea's
Abysmal calm. One solitary bird
Calls from far time and other boughs than these;
But the remembering silence sleeps, unstirred.
All seems achieved, dried up the source of things.
Or is the world too weary to invite
Winters unborn and bid the latent springs
Break out in flower, in fragrance, voice and light?
June once was here; in this autumnal amber
Lingers intangible the small clear trace
Of his ephemeral flight, for ever still.
No more to hope, but only to remember: –
Let there be silence round the slumbering will,
And if time beckons, turn away your face.

APENNINE

In this parcht Apennine the sheep-bells must
Serve with their tinkling for the liquid lapse
And coolness, even in the noonday dust,
Of absent streams – more liquidly, perhaps,
Than water's self, if water were to gush
Between the dry ribs of these bleaching hills:
For in the womb of every pregnant hush
A music sleeps; and when some phantom tills,

157

Arabia's punctual blossoming discloses
Hues more than earthly, iris and evening gold.
But vain those fountains, vain the ethereal roses!
There breathes no fragrance but of roots and mould,
No quenching flows but in those humbler streams
Whose source is earth, is earth and not our dreams.

"Apennine" was originally printed in 91 copies by James and Hilda Wells
(Gaylordsville: Slide Mountain Press, 1930). The last eight lines of this 1930
version are as follows:

> For of all silence the most pregnant hush
> Is music, and the waste that Fancy tills
> Breeds heavenly flowers . . . but flowers for our delight
> Sometimes too pure, of too celestial birth.
> For in rich Fancy's and in art's despite
> There blows no fragrance but of alien earth,
>   No quenching flows but in the humble streams
>   Whose source is earth, is earth, and not our dreams.

ALMERIA

Winds have no moving emblems here, but scour
A vacant darkness, an untempered light;
No branches bend, never a tortured flower
Shudders, root-weary, on the verge of flight;
Winged future, withered past, no seeds nor leaves
Attest those swift invisible feet: they run
Free through a naked land, whose breast receives
All the fierce ardour of a naked sun.
You have the Light for lover. Fortunate Earth!
Conceive the fruit of his divine desire.
But the dry dust is all she brings to birth,
That child of clay by even celestial fire.
Then come, soft rain and tender clouds, abate
This shining love that has the force of hate.

PAGAN YEAR

Heaven's eyes are shut, but cannot wholly kill
The colours of the winter world. Suppressed
And yet how strong, shining in secret, still
Cinder and brooding sable and plum attest
The absent Light. He with his longed rebirth
Unclots the world to an airy dream of leaves;
Shines on; the thin dream ripens into earth,
And the huge elms hang dark above the sheaves.
Magical autumn! All the woods are foxes,
Dozing outstretched in the almost silvery sun.
Oh, bright sad woods and melancholy sky,
Is there no cure for beauty but to run
Yet faster as faster flee hours, flowers and doxies
And dying music, until we also die?

ARMOUR

Crabs in their shells, because they cannot play
Don Juan or the flageolet, are safe;
And every stout Sir Roger, stout Sir Ralph,
Every Black Prince, Bayard and Bourchier may
(Their ribs and rumps hermetically canned)
Securely laugh at arrow, sword and mace.
But in their polished and annealed embrace,
Beneath their iron kiss and iron hand,
The soft defenceless lips and flowery breast,
The tender, tender belly of love receive
From helm and clasping cop and urgent greave
So deep a bruise that, mortally possessed,
Love dies. Only the vulnerable will
Holds what it takes and, holding, does not kill.

SHEEP

Seeing a country churchyard, when the grey
Monuments walked, I with a second glance,
Doubting, postponed the apparent judgment day
To watch instead the random slow advance
Across the down of a hundred nibbling sheep.
And yet these tombs, half fancied and half seen
In the dim world between waking and sleep,
These headstones browsing on their plot of green,
Were sheep indeed and emblems of all life.
For man to dust, dust turns to grass, and grass
Grows wool and feeds on grass. The butcher's knife
Works magic, and the ephemeral sheep forms pass
Through swift tombs and through silent tombs, until
Once more God's acre feeds across the hill.

BLACK COUNTRY

Count yourselves happy that you are not rewarded
For your deserts with brimstone from on high.
Mean, mean among the slag-heaps, mean and sordid,
Your smoking town proclaims its blasphemy.
And yet, too merciful, the offended light
Forgives not only, but with vesperal gold
And roses of the sun repays your spite.
Shining transfigured in the Northern cold,
Instead of chimneys rise Italian towers,
While temples at their feet, not factories, shine;
And like the yet unbodied dream of flowers
Hangs the flushed smoke, through which these eyes divine
Enormous gestures of the gods' fierce wooing,
The nacreous flights, the limbs of bronze pursuing.

CARPE NOCTEM

There is no future, there is no more past,
No roots nor fruits, but momentary flowers.
Lie still, only lie still and night will last,
Silent and dark, not for a space of hours,
But everlastingly. Let me forget
All but your perfume, every night but this,
The shame, the fruitless weeping, the regret.
Only lie still: this faint and quiet bliss
Shall flower upon the brink of sleep and spread,
Till there is nothing else but you and I
Clasped in a timeless silence. But like one
Who, doomed to die, at morning will be dead,
I know, though night seem dateless, that the sky
Must brighten soon before to-morrow's sun.

THE PERGOLA

Pillars, round which the wooden serpents clamber
Towards their own leaves, support the emerald shade,
The eyes, the amethysts, the clustered amber,
That weave the ceiling of this colonnade.
How many thousand Tyrrhenian Septembers
Muskily ripen in a sun-warmed skin!
With all my autumns. For this tongue remembers
Grapes that made sweet a sick child's medicine,
Grapes of the South and of the submarine
Dusk of an English hot-house. But when night
Lids every shining glance of sky between
Leaves now extinct, groping, bereft of sight,
I reach for grapes, but from an inward vine
Pluck sea-cold nipples, still bedewed with brine.

LINES

All day the wheels turn;
All day long the roaring of wheels, the rasping
Weave their imprisoning lattices of noise,
And hammers, hammers in the substance of the world
Carve out another cavernous world, a narrow
Sepulchre, and seal it from the sky,
Lord, with how great a stone!

Only a little beyond the factory walls
Silence is a flawless bowl of crystal,
Brimming, brimming with who can say beforehand,
Who can, returning, even remember what
Beautiful secret. Only a little beyond
These hateful walls the birds among the branches
Secretly come and go.

Time also sleeps, but on the darkening threshold
Of each eternity pauses a moment
And still is time, but empty; still is time,
And therefore knows his emptiness.
The walls are crumbled, the stone is rolled away
(Is there one within? is there a resurrection?);
Stars through the ruined lattices bear witness,
Bear further witness to the further silence,
Witness to the night.

Night is pregnant; silence, alive with voices;
The fullness of the tomb is but corruption;
Only the lifted stone invites the messengers,
Only the empty sepulchre, and only
Now and then, evokes
That from which from the sepulchre arises.

Shy strangers, visiting feet came softly treading,
Came very softly sometimes in the darkness,
Oh, of what far nights and distant tombs!

Came suddenly into the empty time,
Came secretly and lingered secretly,
And through the unsealed door
Beckoned me on to follow.

I have made time empty again; empty, it invites them;
They do not come; have rolled away the stone,
But lie unrisen, lie unvisited.
Merciful God, bid them to come again!
Sometimes in winter
Sea-birds follow the plough,
And the bare field is all alive with wings,
With their white wings and unafraid alightings,
Sometimes in winter. And will they come again?

THE CICADAS

Sightless, I breathe and touch; this night of pines
Is needly, resinous and rough with bark.
Through every crevice in the tangible dark
The moonlessness above it all but shines.

Limp hangs the leafy sky; never a breeze
Stirs, nor a foot in all this sleeping ground;
And there is silence underneath the trees –
The living silence of continuous sound.

For like inveterate remorse, like shrill
Delirium throbbing in the fevered brain,
An unseen people of cicadas fill
Night with their one harsh note, again, again.

Again, again, with what insensate zest!
What fury of persistence, hour by hour!
Filled with what devil that denies them rest,
Drunk with what source of pleasure and of power!

Life is their madness, life that all night long
Bids them to sing and sing, they know not why;
Mad cause and senseless burden of their song;
For life commands, and Life! is all their cry.

I hear them sing, who in the double night
Of clouds and branches fancied that I went
Through my own spirit's dark discouragement,
Deprived of inward as of outward sight:

Who, seeking, even as here in the wild wood,
A lamp to beckon through my tangled fate,
Found only darkness and, disconsolate,
Mourned the lost purpose and the vanished good.

Now in my empty heart the crickets' shout
Re-echoing denies and still denies
With stubborn folly all my learned doubt,
In madness more than I in reason wise.

Life, life! The word is magical. They sing,
And in my darkened soul the great sun shines;
My fancy blossoms with remembered spring,
And all my autumns ripen on the vines.

Life! and each knuckle of the fig-tree's pale
Dead skeleton breaks out with emerald fire.
Life! and the tulips blow, the nightingale
Calls back the rose, calls back the old desire:

And old desire that is for ever new,
Desire, life's earliest and latest birth,
Life's instrument to suffer and to do,
Springs with the roses from the teeming earth;

Desire that from the world's bright body strips
Deforming time and makes each kiss the first;
That gives to hearts, to satiated lips
The endless bounty of to-morrow's thirst.

Time passes, and the watery moonrise peers
Between the tree-trunks. But no outer light
Tempers the chances of our groping years,
No moon beyond our labyrinthine night.

Clueless we go; but I have heard thy voice,
Divine Unreason! harping in the leaves,
And grieve no more; for wisdom never grieves,
And thou hast taught me wisdom; I rejoice.

THE YELLOW MUSTARD

Cabined beneath low vaults of cloud,
    Sultry and still, the fields do lie,
Like one wrapt living in his shroud,
    Who stifles silently.

Stripped of all beauty not their own –
    The gulfs of shade, the golden bloom –
Grey mountain-heaps of slag and stone
    Wall in the silent tomb.

I, through this emblem of a mind
    Dark with repinings, slowly went,
Its captive, and myself confined
    In like discouragement.

When, at a winding of the way,
    A sudden glory met my eye,
As though a single, conquering ray
    Had rent the cloudy sky

And touched, transfiguringly bright
    In that dull plain, one luminous field;
And there the miracle of light
    Lay goldenly revealed.

And yet the reasons for despair
   Hung dark, without one rift of blue;
No loophole to the living air
   Had let the glory through.

In their own soil those acres found
   The sunlight of a flowering weed;
For still there sleeps in every ground
   Some grain of mustard seed.

"The Yellow Mustard" appeared in *Vedanta and the West*, IV (Sept.–Oct., 1941), 14, and was reprinted in Christopher Isherwood's edition of selections from that magazine entitled *Vedanta for the Western World* (Hollywood: Marcel Rodd, 1945).

TITLE INDEX

Alien, The, 60
Almeria, 158
Anniversaries, 57
Apennine, 157
L'Après-Midi d'un Faune (from the French of Stéphane Mallarmé), 76
Arabia Infelix, 143
Armour, 159
Autumn Stillness, 157

Birth of God, The, 98
Black Country, 160
Books and Thoughts, 24
Burning Wheel, The, 15
By the Fire, 62

Caligula or the Triumph of Beauty, 136
Canal, The, 26
Carpe Noctem, 161
Choice, The, 29
Cicadas, The, 163
Complaint, 32
Complaint of a Poet Manqué, 69
"Contrary to Nature and Aristotle", 25
Crapulous Impression, 68

Darkness, 17
Decameron, The, 67
Defeat of Youth, The, 41
Doors of the Temple, 16

Elms, The, 55
Escape, 25

Femmes Damnées (from the French of Charles Baudelaire), 140

Fête Nationale, 156
Fifth Philosopher's Song, 106
First Philosopher's Song, 105
Flowers, The, 54
Formal Verses, 31
Fragment, 33
Frascati's, 109
From the Pillar, 101

Garden, The, 26

Higher Sensualism, The, 29

Ideal Found Wanting, The, 27
In Uncertainty to a Lady, 67
Inspiration, 57
Italy, 59

Jonah, 102

Leda, 83
Life and Art, 104
Life Theoretic, The, 69
Lines ("All day the wheels turn ..."), 162
Louse-Hunters, The (from the French of Arthur Rimbaud), 79
Love Song, 65

Male and Female Created He Them, 100
Meditation, 152
Mediterranean, 155
Melody by Scarlatti, A, 103
Midsummer Day, 156
Minoan Porcelain, 66
Mirror, The, 21
Misplaced Love, 27

Mole, 17
Moor, The, 145
Morning Scene, 108
Mythological Incident, 139

Nero and Sporus or the Triumph of
    Art, 137
Nero and Sporus II, 139
Ninth Philosopher's Song, 107
Noblest Romans, 147

On Hampstead Heath, 100
On the Bus, 71
Orion, 148
Out of the Window, 56

Pagan Year, 159
Panic, 71
Pergola, The, 161
Perils of the Small Hours, 31
Philoclea in the Forest, 22
Picture by Goya: A Highway Rob-
    bery, 135
Poem, 73
Points and Lines, 71
Private Property, 65

Quotidian Vision, 20

Reef, The, 52
Return from Business, 72
Return to an Old Home, 33
Revelation, 66

Scenes of the Mind, 74
Seasons, 154
Second Philosopher's Song, 106

Sententious Song (see footnote to
    Ninth Philosopher's Song), 107
Sentimental Summer, 28
September, 153
Sheep, 160
Social Amenities, 70
Soles Occidere et Redire Possunt
    (Foreword by Huxley), 109
Song of Poplars, 51
Sonnet ("If that a sparkle . . ."), 30
Sonnet ("Were I to die . . . "), 28
Stanzas, 72
Storm at Night, 154

Summer Stillness, 57
Sunset, A, 103
Sympathy, 100

Theatre of Varieties, 131
Tide, 155
Topiary, 70
Two Realities, 20
Two Seasons, The, 19

Valedictory, 63
Variations on a Theme, 103
Variations on a Theme of Laforgue,
    22
Verrey's, 108
Villiers de l'Isle-Adam, 16
Vision, 21

Waking, 61
Walk, The, 34
Wheel, The (earlier title of "The
    Burning Wheel"), 16
Winter Dream, 54

Yellow Mustard, The, 165